Would you like to spend
house?

Would you like to know how to gain a positively unfair advantage over other buyers?

If you don't start now, what will the consequences be in five years' time or in 10 years' time?

Buying Your First Home

The 7-Step Plan to Go From Renting to Owning a House

Tamara Blackmiller

Contents

To Buy or Not to Buy...**13**

Do you Want to Make your Life Better? 13

How to Use this Book 16

Disclaimer 17

Why are People Buying?...**21**

Buy or Rent? Three Boys Case Study 21

Buy or Rent? Three Girls Case Study 23

3-Step Property Ladder Case Study............................... 26

Other Reasons to Buy 29

Step 1: Finances **33**

How Much Money Can You Get? 34

How much cash do you need? 36

What if my salary is not enough? 37

Other Purchase Costs... 38

When to Pay it? 40

How to Save Money for the Deposit? 42

Step 2: Check and Build Credit History Early....................**51**

Where the Information Comes From 51

Records That Are not in the Credit File 52

How to Improve your Credit Score: Dos and Don'ts 53

The Impact of Student Loan 59

Step 3: Mortgages **63**

Government Help-to-Buy Schemes 64

1. Help to Buy: Equity Loan 65

2. Mortgage Guarantee Scheme 67

3. Shared Ownership Scheme.. 68

4. Right to Buy... 70

How to Find a Mortgage Broker 72

What Mortgage to Choose? 74

What Do Banks Require? 79

Self-Employed Options 83

Step 4: How to Find Your House.................................**87**

Start Online so you Know the Area Well 87
What to Look for in an Area 89
How to Compare and What to Choose...92
Using a Buying Agent 95
Buying at Auctions...95

Step 5: Viewings.. 99

What to Look for During Viewings? 101
Questions to Ask the Agent During the Viewing 103
Estimating the House Value 107
How to Choose..109
Making an Offer 111
Some Tips 113
Staying out of the Crowd Can Give an Unfair Advantage 115

Step 6: Conveyancing – Legal Process................................ 119

So What's Next? 119
How to Find a Solicitor 122
What Solicitors Do 123
What Can Go Wrong?...126
Exchange-Completion 130

Step 7: You Get the Keys.. 137

Happily Ever After.. 147

What Could Go Wrong and How to Reduce the Risk? 147
Financial Planning...151
What Taxes Affect Properties? 154

Chain of Actions... 159

Buying Your First House in 100 Words.............................. 163

Acknowledgements 165

Moving Forward.. 167

Appendix 1: Stamp Duty Land Tax 169

Appendix 2: Average Cost of Renting vs Buying by Region
.... 171

Appendix 3: Renting vs Buying 173

Appendix 4: 3-Step Property Ladder 177

Appendix 5: Mortgage Rates..181

Appendix 6: References and Useful Resources..................185

References 185

Appendix 7: Glossary..191

Index...203

Free Gifts!

As a thank-you for getting this book, I'd like to give you some free gifts:

- A spreadsheet for analysis of houses so it's easier to compare and make your important decision.
- A spreadsheet for recording your expenses and your progress with savings and wealth growth.
- Useful checklists for your move.
- To avoid typing long links for resources you can download them from the website

Go to the link here:

https://buyfirsthome.co.uk/FreeGifts/

...or you can scan this QR code using your mobile

Free Gifts

Resource List

Check also useful information and what help you can get on https://buyfirsthome.co.uk/

Enjoy!

To Buy or Not to Buy

To Buy or Not to Buy

"The best thing to do is get started and modify as you go along."

Simon Chaplin, Banish the Bottleneck

Do you Want to Make your Life Better?

Whether to buy your own house or not is mostly a personal choice. If you have opened this book, most likely you are considering buying a house. Regardless of what you may read in the media, I strongly believe that everybody can buy a property. It can take some time and effort, but you just need to know how to do it. The first house is the most difficult, others will be easier.

If you want your own place but you don't know where to start, this book is for you.

I can understand how desperate you might feel trying to find a way to get your own property. I still remember my feelings many years ago when my husband and I had no other choice but to live with my parents after we were married. They had a small, 1-bedroom apartment, and my young husband joined me in my 7 square-meters room. It took us seven long years to find the money and the opportunity and move to our own place. During these years our first son was born, and with three of us in the same room, we felt more and more pressure to get out. My loving parents were very understanding and provided a huge amount of help with our toddler. But five people were way too many for this tiny space. We had no freedom or privacy; we were just surviving and dreaming about our own place.

We would be happy to move anywhere—to a tiny studio, to a remote place—as long as we were on our own. We had no money for the furniture, and we were prepared to sleep on the floor in our sleeping bags. Anything!

Living with parents as well as several temporary jobs certainly helped us to save enough money for our first house deposit, but this came in exchange for massive inconvenience and loss of freedom. Even with a very loving family, it's not easy to live with three generations in a very small place, everybody with their own schedule, needs, and demands. We were lucky that we still had our family connections after we eventually moved out to our own apartment. After this experience, I strongly believe that young families should have their own space as soon as possible and love their parents from a distance—at least more than a few meters!

We didn't have much furniture at the beginning, and we needed to do some decoration, but even now I remember our excitement when we saw our very own empty space with the smell of fresh paint. This was the beginning of a wonderful new life; we were confident that we could overcome all obstacles and achieve everything.

It took us seven years to move to our own place, but many people can do it much quicker in the UK now. Yes, house prices keep going up. After you buy your own property, you will be delighted to see that the value of your house goes up as well. But to benefit from that, you better do your first step as soon as possible, as it will not be getting easier.

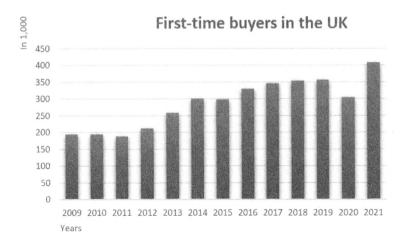

Source: Statista

Figure 1: Numbers of first-time buyers in the UK 2009-2020

According to Statista [1], in recent years, more than 300,000 properties were sold annually to the first-time buyers. Even in 2020 there were 304,660 first-time buyers, despite the impact of Covid-19, and 2021 saw a big increase to 409,370.

If they can do it, you can do it too. Why not try?

For some people it can take several months, while for others it could take several years before everything is ready. It's is your choice; if you really want to buy your own home, this book will show you how you can do it too.

A high salary and a big deposit certainly help, but there are solutions for everybody, and this book will give you the tools you need to start your new, exciting project.

There may be obstacles and sacrifices, and it will take time. But people who are prepared, do it quicker. Your second

15

house will take much less time when you are ready to move again.

What do you think will happen in 10 years' time if you do nothing now? Every year there will be someone moving to their own place. After 10 years half of your friends—or more—will have their own houses. Do you want to be in the bottom half envying them?

Your actions now will determine your success. We all dream about having something nice, or doing something we wish to do, but it's still daydreaming until we take the first action, then the next, until we create a chain of actions.

Buying your first property is a big project that is full of uncertainty, and it can't be finished in one day, however hard you work on that one day. At the end of this book is a chain of actions. You can either choose to follow them in order, or you can just choose one of them, which is easier for you. Just start your first action.

How to Use this Book

To buy just any house is not that difficult. What is more difficult is to avoid mistakes or problems which can cost you a lot of time and money.

You need a basic understanding of how numbers work, and I have provided detailed examples to help you. Success in properties very much depends on numbers, but don't be afraid of it, as most calculations in finance are adding and subtracting, sometimes multiplying, any kid can do it. Even if you didn't like maths at school, if you slowly follow the examples, and as it becomes familiar, it will be much easier as all the calculations are the same. But you will need to know how it works because you will do similar calculations when you do your own analysis before buying.

Not everybody likes numbers, so the more boring stuff is in the Appendices, do look there, the information could be useful.

People in properties use a lot of jargon. From reading newspapers and online, we know most of it, but there might still be some terms that you don't know the meaning of. The Glossary in Appendix 7 provides explanations of jargon, for example, what is freehold or leasehold.

If there is still something that I missed and you would like to know, send me an email to book@buyfirsthome.co.uk, I'll be very happy to hear about your suggestions and comments.

Disclaimer

This book is not intended to give legal, financial or investment advice. It's for information and education purposes only. All efforts have been made to check the accuracy of the content at the time of publishing, but rules and legislation can change quickly. Therefore you should consult independent advisers before making the decision to buy a house.

Why are People Buying?

Why are People Buying?

"You don't have to see the whole staircase, just take the first step"

Martin Luther King, Jr

There are good financial reasons to buy a house now: interest rates for mortgages are at a very low level, and there is a good chance that the interest rate will stay low for some time. Low interest rates mean that mortgage payments could be lower than rent, even with capital repayments.

Homeowners are more than £800 a year better off than renters, according to a Which? magazine report [2], and in London, the difference reaches £4,600. Appendix 2 provides a comparison between different regions.

These are just average figures, but the situation can work out to be even more advantageous for many people, as you can see from the examples below.

Buy or Rent? Three Boys Case Study

To compare what happens over 5 years, we use real prices on the market that are available now, as well as the mortgages that are currently available. You can see further details of these examples in Appendix 3, do not just believe me, follow my calculations there; it will give you a real advantage if you understand how the numbers work.

This is a brief summary.

Case Study 1: Three Boys

South West London

Three friends were discussing that they are fed up with renting. They want to buy, but it would involve some sacrifices to save the money for the deposit.

David has decided that he wants to enjoy his life and he doesn't want to restrict himself, so he will just continue renting 1-bedroom flat. His rent is £1,200 per month. He is lucky that his landlord hasn't increased the rent, so David stays in the same place and pays the same amount for 5 years. The total amount he pays for rent over 5 years is £72,000.

Neil doesn't have a big deposit and his money is restricted, so he decides to go for the cheapest option. He buys a 1-bedroom flat for £300,000. He pays a 5% deposit of £15,000 and takes a 2-year fixed mortgage at a 2.95% interest rate. After 2 years he re-mortgages to 3-year fixed rate, taking a 90% LTV (Loan-To-Value) mortgage with 2.12% interest. Over 5 years he pays total interest of £33,027, and at the end of the fifth year, he has an outstanding mortgage of £250,047.

Tom has a bit more money for the deposit, and he decides to take the government 40% loan, which is interest-free for the first 5 years, but for this, he needs to buy a new apartment. He finds a 1-bedroom flat in the same area for £400,000, and he managed to pay a 5% deposit of £20,000. Because he is taking only a 55% LTV mortgage due to the

---

government loan of 40%, his interest rate for the fixed-rate 5-year mortgage is lower, at only 1.4%. During these 5 years he pays £14,380 interest, and at the end, he had outstanding mortgage of £189,440 plus the government loan £160,000.

Note: Both Neil and Tom will need additional money to pay for other buying costs.

Table 1: Boys results

	Deposit	Spent on rent or interest	Saved over 5 years	Saving to deposit ratio
David	no house	£72,000		
Neil	£15,000	£28,796	£43,204	2.9 times
Tom	£20,000	£17,345	£54,655	2.7 times

Buy or Rent? Three Girls Case Study

Case Study 2: Three Girls

Outside London

Here there were also three friends who were discussing how they could buy their homes. House prices are cheaper here, but salaries are lower too, so not everyone will be able to buy.

Jane has decided that she wants to enjoy her life, so she will just continue renting 1-bedroom apartment. Her rent is £525 per month, and she is also lucky with a kind landlord—no rent increase in 5 years. So, Jane stays in the same place and pays the same amount for 5 years. The total amount she pays in rent during the 5 years is £31,500.

Linda doesn't have a big deposit, so she decides to buy the cheapest 1-bedroom apartment she can find. She finds one to buy for £100,000; she pays a 5% deposit of £5,000 and takes a 2-year fixed mortgage at a 2.95% interest rate. After 2 years, she re-mortgages to a 3-year fixed-rate taking a 90% LTV mortgage with 2.12% interest. Over the 5 years she pays total interest of £11,009; and at the end of the fifth year, she has an outstanding mortgage of £83,349.

Amanda had a bit more money for the deposit, so she decides to take the government 20% loan. But for this, she needs to buy a new-build flat. She finds a 1-bedroom flat in the same area for £160,000, and she pays a 5% deposit of £8,000. She also takes a 75% LTV mortgage. The interest rate for a fixed-rate 5-year mortgage is 1.63%, and over the 5 years, she pays £16,163 interest. In the end, she has an outstanding mortgage of £103,837 plus a government loan of £32,000.

Note: Linda and Amanda also will need additional money to pay for other buying costs.

Table 2: Girls results

	Deposit	Spent on rent or interest	Saved over 5 years	Saving to deposit ratio
Jane	no house	£31,500		
Linda	£5,000	£8,039	£23,461	4.7 times
Amanda	£8,000	£9,467	£22,033	2.8 times

Analysis

Let us see who is better off.

In both examples, David and Jane, who were renting, spent much more money, and they have no houses at the end, so no opportunity for further savings. They were lucky that their rent didn't increase, but during a 5-year period a rent increase is quite possible, especially if they move to another place, so the savings when buying your own place would be even greater, even without taking into account the potential increase in house prices.

Neil, Tom, Linda and Amanda, who bought their own places, saved a considerable amount of money and they have their own houses, which will grow in value, and they will continue saving compared to rents. Their savings differ, and although the London saving figures look higher in money terms, if we take into account what was spent on the deposits, Linda has the biggest increase. Yes, she needed to save £5,000 for the deposit, but after 5 years she saved £23,461 on rent payments, which is 4.7 times increase compared to her initial deposit of £5,000. And this is even before we take into account increase in house prices.

It's not clear how it can be compared in 10 years' time when house value growth would need to be taken into account too. Very often the value of new builds does not grow as fast as it does for houses on the secondary market. Also, after 5 years Tom and Amanda will have to start paying the interest on the government loan; and if they sell, they will be required to pay the government a proportion of price increase. This will be covered in more detail later in the book, in Step 3 Mortgages.

These examples are for illustration purposes only, and your local situation could be different. In these examples monthly mortgage payments are lower than monthly rent. There might be areas where rent is lower, but it will still result in being greater than the interest part of the mortgage payment due to very low current mortgage rates on the market. If you want to achieve bigger savings, do a similar analysis for options in your area.

The good news is that you can save a lot of money if you buy your own place to live in instead of paying the rent.

3-Step Property Ladder Case Study

People over many generations have been able to considerably increase their wealth through properties as house prices have risen by 5% every year, on average. Nobody can predict what will happen with house prices next year, or in 5 or in 10 years, but due to very low current interest rates you can save a lot of money in the long run by having your own place.

The good news is that it can work even better now due to very low interest rates, as you can see in the example below.

---

3 Steps Property Ladder Case Study

Mary has managed to save £7,000, which she hopes can help her to buy her own place. She has found a 1-bedroom apartment for £100,000 and used £5,000 as the deposit, with the rest to cover other expenses. A bank agreed to lend her £95,000 as a 5-year fixed-rate repayment mortgage.

She develops the following plan for how she can move along the property ladder:

At the end of the 5th year, her outstanding mortgage will be £83,737. Assuming that property prices go up annually by 5% (which is a relatively prudent estimate), her property will have a value of £127,600.

If she sells her first flat for this amount, Mary will have over £43,000 in equity, which would be enough to buy a bigger property for £170,000 and take a 75% LTV mortgage of £127,500.

After the end of the next 5th year (10th year from the first purchase), she will have an outstanding mortgage of £110,465. So, if the property prices increase by an average of 5% again, her house will have a value of almost £217,000 and her equity will grow to an amazing £106,500.

This will be enough to sell again and buy a much bigger detached house in her area for £420,000 with a 25% deposit and 5-year fixed-rate mortgage.

At the end of this period (15th year from the first purchase) Mary's equity will grow to £262,000.

See what happens? You can grow your money a lot.

Yes, the money is in equity, but it's still your money, and there are different ways to use it.

In just 10 years, Mary's money can grow from an initial £7,000 to over £262,000 in equity after 15 years.

Who can save so much money while renting?

To see more details about Mary's calculations, please look at Appendix 4.

Certainly, Mary made many assumptions. She assumed that

property prices would continue growing, that interest rates would stay low, and that her salary would grow enough so the bank would be willing to give her bigger mortgages. But would you be satisfied to have £100,000 not in 10 years, but in 15 years? Still not bad?

Table 3 Overpaying mortgage by £100 per month

Years	Payments/ Additional Equity	Interest saving		
		2%	3%	4%
10	£12,000	£1,390	£2,160	£2,990
15	£18,000	£3,151	£4,961	£6,989
25	£30,000	£9,291	£15,150	£21,980

If Mary continues prudent savings and overpays the mortgage by just £100 per month, she can save on mortgage interest and increase her equity even more. See Table 3.

This is a hypothetical example, as we certainly can't predict future house prices and future interest rates, but this estimation is based on historic and current figures. The actual figures could be worse, but they could be better. This 5% of annual growth, which we used in the example, would give the house price only £162,900 for the first house, but we know that in many areas house prices can double during a 10-year period.

Also, over a 10-to-15-year period people gain considerable work experience, they acquire new skills, they build their reputation and respect, which will likely result in salary growth. In many professions it's not unusual to double your salary over 10–15 years, making further savings and wealth growth.

Other Reasons to Buy

Financial reasons work very well for buying, but there are other considerations too.

If you have your home:

- Nobody can take it from you and push you out if you pay your monthly mortgage payments.
- You can save a lot every year instead of paying rent. When you pay rent the money goes into the pockets of landlords, and it's lost for you forever.
- In your own house you have much more freedom to adjust your house to your own needs; you could paint the walls in red and black if you want, or decorate in any way you like, and you can also look after your home much better.
- It's said that your home is your castle, therefore nobody can enter it without your permission. In contrast, landlords can request entry at almost any time, and often it happens at the most inconvenient moments when you are busy with something else.
- House prices can go up and down, but your rent only goes up, leaving less in your own pocket.
- You can make improvements to your house that cause the value of the house to increase considerably more than the money you have spent.
  When you pay off the mortgage, your monthly living costs will be considerably reduced—no rent, no mortgage—which is especially good at an older age when your earning will most likely decrease.

29

> ## Do it now!
>
> Write down your three most important reasons to buy

- This is your legacy, you can pass the property to your children or grandchildren when you die, your asset will stay in the family and improve the lives of those that come after you. If you are renting, there is nothing to pass on.
- You can cash in on the increased equity in your house and use it for something else, for example for buying another house, or travelling the world.

Step 1: Finances

Step 1: Finances

"Do not save what is left after spending, but spend what is left after saving."   Warren Buffet

Unlike buying just about anything else, you can't wait for a Christmas sale to buy a house with a 70% discount. House prices might go down occasionally, but not as much, a more likely reduction will be 10–20%. Also, unlike a Christmas sale, nobody knows when it might happen; you might have to wait for 5–10 years for the next property crash to take advantage of it. You will save more during these years simply by replacing paying rent by paying a mortgage instead. If a price correction does happen in the property market, you can use this opportunity to jump to another step of your property ladder.

To begin, you will need a certain amount of money. The good news is that it might be much less than you think. This chapter is about how much and how to get it.

You do need to find where to get the finances to cover the cost of the house—and even more, as there are some additional expenses accrued in the process of buying. Some of the money can come from a bank as a mortgage (which we will discuss in greater detail later), but you will still need the money for the deposit and other costs.

It's always a good idea to plan and manage your finances well if you don't want to still be counting every penny before your next salary in your 40s and even 50s. I haven't heard about anybody wealthy enough, who can't manage their money, and it's especially useful to start planning your money in advance if you are thinking about buying your first house.

There are two important figures which you need to understand:

1) how much you can borrow
2) how much you need for the deposit

In the good old days, you could buy a house with a 100% mortgage, needing none of your own money, and there were mortgages available with interest-only payments. Now you need at least a 5% deposit and there are restrictions on how much money you can borrow, depending on your salary, credit score, and your circumstances.

How Much Money Can You Get?

There will be more in Step 3 about mortgages, how much money you can borrow, and how much you can get from government schemes. But for now, a rough estimation you can use to define your expectations is to multiply your salary by 4.5 (combined salary with your partner if you are buying with someone else) to see how much mortgage you can get. Different banks might have additional requirements, and some might give you even more, but multiplying by 4.5 is a good starting point.

If your salary is £20,000 per year, you can borrow £20,000 x 4.5 = £90,000 from a bank, which would be 95% of the price of a house costing about £94,750. You will need to have a 5% deposit totalling £4,738, plus other purchase costs.

Table 4 shows some examples. According to ONS (the Office of National Statistics), in 2020 the average salary in the UK was £38,600 per year, see what you can buy with it in the line in bold.

Table 4: What can you buy for your salary?

Salary	How much to borrow Salary x 4.5	House price if take mortgage 95%	Deposit 5%	House price if take mortgage 90%	Deposit 10%
£20.00	£90,000	£94,737	£4,737	£100,000	£10,000
£30,000	£135,000	£142,105	£7,105	£150,000	£15,000
£38,000	**£171,000**	**£180,000**	**£9,000**	**£190,000**	**£19,000**
£50.00	£225,000	£236,842	£11,842	£250,000	£25,000
£70,000	£315,000	£331,579	£16,579	£350,000	£35,000
£90,000	£405,000	£426,316	£21,316	£450,000	£45,000

If you have a salary of £30,000, can you find something in your area for £142,000?

If you live in London and have a salary of £50,000, can you find something for £236,000?

Or to look at it from another angle, see Table 5: What salary do you need to buy a house in your area?

Table 5: How much income do you need to buy a house in your area?

House price	Deposit 5% required	Mortgage 95% LTV	Required income	Deposit 10% required	Mortgage 90% LTV	Required income
80,000	4,000	76,000	16,889	8,000	72,000	16,000
100,000	5,000	95,000	21,111	10,000	90,000	20,000
150,000	7,500	142,500	31,667	15,000	135,000	30,000
200,000	10,000	190,000	42,222	20,000	180,000	40,000
250,000	12,500	237,500	52,778	25,000	225,000	50,000
300,000	15,000	285,000	63,333	30,000	270,000	60,000
400,000	20,000	380,000	84,444	40,000	360,000	80,000
450,000	22,500	427,500	95,000	45,000	405,000	90,000

In London house price growth was much higher than salary growth for many years, which makes it especially difficult for first-time buyers to buy in London, but in some areas, houses are within reach for a person with an average salary. Zoopla research [3] reveals the 10 most affordable places to live in the UK, where the mortgage one can get with an average salary is much greater than the average house price.

How much cash do you need?

So, for the second question: 'How much cash do I need?', the simple answer is: at least 5% of the house price, plus buying expenses, but it might get more complicated when we look at the details.

Depending on your salary, as shown in Table 4, you can estimate what deposit you need. Saving for a 10% deposit could take longer, but it will considerably increase the options available to you.

If you're at an early stage of your planning and saving for the deposit, don't be stressed too much if house prices in your area are higher for what you want to buy. Your salary might increase in a couple of years, or you may find some additional income, or house prices could go down for some reason. You just need to be ready with your deposit.

What if my salary is not enough?

There could be other solutions:

- buying with a friend/a partner so you combine the salary to get a bigger mortgage
- you can try to save for a bigger deposit
- ask the bank of mum and dad to help you by giving a gift or a loan
- consider buying a smaller property to start with
- consider looking a bit further outside the city where house prices are cheaper

Just start preparing the money for the deposit, and many obstacles may be overcome, and you will find a solution.

REMEMBER: Even if you can only afford a very small place, or in a cheaper area, it's not forever. The sooner you buy, the more savings you will achieve in the long run. If it's not absolutely your dream house, for example if you want to live closer to your friends or family, you don't need to consider the house you're buying to be the end of the road. Covid-19 might distort this statistic, but historically people move houses every 5–7 years. Your second purchase will be easier, and you don't need to worry much about property prices growing too fast—yours will grow too.

Other Purchase Costs

How much will you need in addition to the deposit?

To make the calculations and examples easier, we will use the round numbers £100,000 and £200,000 as house prices:

Table 6: Cash required to buy a house

		House price	
		£200,000	**£100,000**
1	Deposit 5%	£10,000	£5,000
2	Legal fees plus other conveyancing costs, like searches and transaction fees (more about that in Chapter 4). Very often solicitors will charge higher fees for leasehold properties. This figure is for illustration purposes only; it could be higher or lower, depending on the quotation from your solicitor.	£1,000	£1,000
3	Stamp Duty and Land Tax (SDLT), or equivalent in Scotland and Wales. Please see the table in Appendix 1 for how SDLT is calculated. For our illustration, there is no Stamp Duty, as both examples are below the £300,000 limit for first-time buyers.	£0	£0

4	Mortgage arrangement fees (more about this in Step 3). Additional expenses at this stage: mortgage broker fee, valuation fee, other fees that the bank can charge. Some mortgages don't have an arrangement fee, this usually comes with a higher interest rate, as the fee can be added to the mortgage amount so it doesn't need to be paid at the time of purchase. Also, some banks don't charge for the valuation. We're using the mortgage broker fee only; in most cases, this will be payable only after completion.	£250	£250
5	Property survey costs. These vary depending on the type of the survey but will normally be between £250 and £1,500. This is different from the survey arranged by the bank, and it's discretional. It is advisable to have it to avoid potential big problems with the house (more about this in Step 6). This figure is for illustration purposes, and it could be higher, but you might not need it for a new build.	£360	£360
6	Moving costs. If you don't have much to move, and your friends or relatives can help you, the cost could be zero. But then you need to buy at least some furniture. If you already have your own furniture, this cost could be even higher, so do plan at least something here.	£250	£250

7	Building insurance. For leasehold properties, it might be included in service charges, but if you buy a freehold property, you will need to pay it.	£250	£250
	Total cash required for buying	**£12,110**	**£7,110**

When to Pay it?

Your solicitor will ask you to transfer some money to them as a deposit. It's usually £250–£300, which they will keep as a payment on account. They might keep all or part of it to cover their expenses if your purchase doesn't go through.

REMEMBER: Solicitors will not start their work until you make this payment on account, so do it promptly to avoid delays.

Another early payment will be for the survey, if you have decided to have one. It's better to do it at the early stages because the result might show that something is wrong with the property, and you might want to renegotiate the price or pull out completely if you don't want to deal with problems. This doesn't happen often, but it does happen.

You will need to transfer the costs in rows 1–3 from Table 4 to your solicitor on or before the day of exchange of contracts. Your solicitor will send you a statement with all expenses showing how much to pay.

Brokers usually invoice soon after the purchase is complete, and you pay removal costs before or on the day of your moving.

There could be other costs, like refurbishment, buying furniture and new stuff for the house, but most will be discretional and more flexible with the timing.

Building insurance should be paid on or before the date of exchange of contracts, but it can be paid by a credit card.

TIP: When you plan your finances, add some additional funds. If you don't spend it, it will stay with you and you won't have lost anything. But it might be very valuable to have on hand if you urgently need something extra.

When you have your target budget for the deposit and other costs, you'll need to save the money from your salary or ask mum and dad for help. When looking at your finances, if you think it can't be achieved in a reasonable time, you just need to adjust the area you're looking in so that you can buy a cheaper house, or you need to plan it over a longer period. At least after considering the steps below and planning your actions, you will know that in X years' time you can make your offer and start the process.

Do it now!

Make a note:

- your current income
- how much mortgage you can get
- house price you can target
- deposit you need

The good news is that if you're determined to buy your own place and you're prepared to put effort into it, most likely you will hit your target earlier. This is because salaries for young people go up quicker than inflation and quicker than average salaries since you will be learning new skills and gaining more experience.

How to Save Money for the Deposit?

If you're at a very early stage of planning and have almost nothing in savings, you need to plan how you can come to the exciting point of having the money ready.

1. The first step is to review what regular income you have and how you spend it. Do you spend all your salary and struggle in the last few days before the next one appears in your bank account?

You need to watch what you're doing and how you spend your money. The easiest way is to record all your spending for some time. Very often, just being aware of your spending helps you to manage your finances better.

You might record your spending for just a couple of months to see the pattern, or you might decide to do it until you buy your home. This is an easy step, and it's completely under your control. There are elements like your current salary, transport costs or other things, which are not under your control. There might even be some additional expenditure you can't control completely, but making notes is something you can do.

You can keep a daily record (advisable), or weekly (you might forget something), or monthly (you do need to keep all receipts and go through your bank and credit card statements, which can be time-consuming). You can do it on paper or computer or on your mobile, and there are some apps for it—just do whatever is easy for you. Start experimenting and see what works better for you.

If it's a completely new habit for you, you can approach it as any other new habit: you need to make it easy, otherwise, you will probably drop it soon, and you need a reminder so you don't forget. It's easier to remember to do a new habit if you combine it with something you already do. For example, if you decide to write down your expenses every day, what about doing it after you have your dinner? Or during your lunch break? Or immediately after you have spent something?

To make it easy, I keep my list where I go most often; in the kitchen or at my desk and with a pen ready to make a note. You will notice it when you're around it, and if you have a pen ready, you can just write down whatever you need to.

If you don't like paper and prefer your phone, one of the options could be to make notes while you commute to work if you're using public transport. There are always minutes here and there when we're waiting for something, and it can be good to pass the time by doing something useful.

You might miss some days in the beginning. Don't let it derail you, just record as much as you remember next time. It will become easier with time. Do praise yourself and feel good every time you've done it—you have accomplished another small step toward your future purchase. You already have your motivation to keep going, you want to buy your house, and this is your first action, which will lead to the chain of other actions!

TIP: If you keep these records, you can provide them to your lender to show them how you spend your money. It will be a strong indicator for them that you do manage your money well!

You will also need to see the pattern of your spending. There's a useful table to help you with this that I have been using for years.

You can download it here for free: https://buyfirsthome.co.uk/FreeGifts/

The table groups unavoidable expenditure, like your transport costs, rent, food and others. There will be other costs which you will also need to keep, such as gym membership. You do want to be healthy and happy. This might be a discretional expenditure, but if it helps you to feel good, be active and be motivated, then it's money well spent.

TIP: If you live with your parents, you can't show the bank that you already have your monthly living expenditure. So you might decide to pay them something towards rent. It's never a bad idea to contribute from time to time, and it will also be nice for your parents. Then when you apply for a mortgage you can show the bank that you have accommodation expenses, and that you plan your monthly living expenditure and manage your finances well.

2. So, what's left? Is there something in the list of expenditure that you can avoid? There are plenty of tips on how to save daily costs, for example, you can have your coffee at home instead of Costa or Starbucks on your way to work. If you like them, treat yourself from time to time to celebrate your efforts when you have some good savings during the month. You will enjoy it more when it has a special meaning to you.

Are you buying too many expensive clothes? You do want to look good; can you achieve it for half of your usual cost?

Any packed lunch would be cheaper than having lunch in a cafe, and even cheaper than a sandwich in Pret a Manger. It could also be a healthier option—a good side effect! Also cooking your dinner is healthier and cheaper than takeaway, at least you know what you are putting there.

3. The first step with saving money is to start with at least something, like saving 10% of your monthly income, for example. Although it might be a little uncomfortable at the beginning, after some time it'll be unnoticeable. Open a separate bank account. It doesn't need to be generating high interest, but if it gives at least something additional, it would be even better. It will give you great satisfaction to see your money grow. Just after you receive your salary, transfer 10% into your savings account. To make it even easier, arrange a Standing Order for the day after you receive each salary payment. I would suggest to start with 10% of your net monthly salary, and when it becomes easier, you can increase the percentage.

If 10% sounds scary and you think it could be too difficult, start with 5% or £10 or £5 or even £1. This must become a habit, so start small and grow it later. Start with another account where you can withdraw the money without a penalty in case of emergency. Easy-access accounts don't usually give high interest rate returns, but this is all about building a habit of saving. We'll discuss generating more income later.

If you have a bonus or salary increase, put it to your savings pot **in full** and celebrate this to feel good about saving. It's much easier to transfer the additional money to another account straight away, you didn't have it before and lived

45

somehow, so you can certainly just continue. Meanwhile, your savings will grow quicker, bringing the big purchase closer and closer.

4. Start planning your monthly expenditure. By now you should know how much you really need, how much you can save and what's left. Try to leave enough money for all necessities, like Direct Debits or transport and food. Plus, I would recommend leaving some additional money for unexpected things so you don't need to take the money from your savings pot. At any rate, it's important to try to avoid ever taking money from your savings. Make it your policy that, in your mind taking money from there is un-acceptable. If at the end of the month you still have something left in this pot for unexpected things, transfer it to the savings account together with your monthly transfer. 'Rinse and repeat'.

Do celebrate if you managed the month without taking anything from your savings account or if you have something additional to transfer. Well done! Treat yourself with something nice so you feel good about your efforts—better that it's not too expensive though.

5. When you have accumulated some money and you have established a saving habit, it's time to think about how your money can generate an additional income. How to invest is a huge topic, and it's outside of the scope of this book, but the main idea is that your money should work for you and generate additional income for you. If you plan that you won't need your money for a long time, the range of available options could be greater. But if you plan

to buy your house and use your money in 1–5 years' time, you need something more reliable where you can get your money back quickly. A simple option is a bank account that generates interest, but unfortunately, due to very low interest rates now, saving accounts don't give big returns. Still, if you put your money into a deposit account, it can generate at least some return. It could be £20–£30–£100 per year depending on your deposit amount; and with current tax rules, it will be tax-free. If you choose a fixed-term account, it will also help you to avoid the temptation to dip into your savings pot.

The biggest boost your money can get is with a Lifetime ISA, a savings scheme where the government adds 25% to your savings. The previous scheme, Help to Buy ISA, was closed to new applicants in November 2019, but if you opened one of those before that, you can still add money there until 2029 — but hopefully, you will be able to buy your house well before that date.

REMEMBER: Do guard your money against loss and avoid any risky investments at this stage.

This is not investment advice, and you should consult with an independent financial adviser, who can give knowledgeable advice based on your specific situation. If you want to educate yourself regarding investments and growing your wealth, you might join the millions of people who read the bestselling book, *"Rich Dad Poor Dad"* by Robert Kiyosaki [4].

6. Why not consider how you can generate additional income? Review what things you have and which of them you don't need. There could be something that other people need and are prepared to pay money for.

Not only can you make more space for yourself by removing the clutter, but you will also need to carry less to your new place, and you can add several hundred pounds to your pot! One of my good friends was very happy to generate a couple of thousand on eBay by selling her unwanted things before Christmas. Christmas time could be especially good for this, but you need to prepare everything well before that.

Step 2: Check and Build Credit History Early

Step 2: Check and Build Credit History Early

"Good preparation is 90% of success."

An old adage

Even if nothing special happened with your credit history, even if you have never used credit cards and never took loans, it's still a good idea to check what your credit score is and what financial details are recorded against your name. Mistakes happen, and building a good credit history can take 2–5 years, so you'd better start as soon as possible.

There are three UK agencies that keep these records and give data to potential lenders when they're considering applications: Experian [5], Equifax [6] and TransUnion [7].

Where the Information Comes From

1. Electoral roll information. This information is publicly available and contains addresses and the names of the people who live at them.

2. Court records. County court records about judgments, decrees, individual voluntary arrangements, bankruptcies and other court debt orders show if a person has a history of debt problems.

3. Search, address and linked data. This includes records of other lenders or companies that have searched a person's file when he/she applied for credit, addresses which are linked to that person and other people who have a financial association with the person.

The big gas and electricity companies do hard credit checks, and these go into the file too.

4. Account data. Banks, utility companies, mobile phone companies and other organisations share details of all account behaviour on credit or store cards, mortgages, loans, bank accounts, utility and mobile phone contracts from the past six years.

Records That Are not in the Credit File

- Medical records. These are confidential and not shared with anyone outside the medical system.
- Saving accounts. Although they show the applicant in a positive light as a financially responsible person, details of savings will not be in the credit history as they are not credit products. It's up to you to make sure you show them to the mortgage lender when the time comes.
- Race, ethnicity, religion and other social details.
- Salary will not be in the credit file, but any credit company will ask about it on the application form. Be consistent, as different figures in different applications can cause confusion and rejection.
- Criminal records are not listed here as opposite to any debt-related convictions, like CCJ (County Court

Judgment for debt) and bankruptcy records, which are in the file.

How to Improve your Credit Score: Dos and Don'ts

You can check your credit history for free, and you'd better do it even before you have the money for the deposit to make sure that there are no unexpected records against your name. Unfortunately, it does happen, and you don't want to find about it when your bank starts doing credit checks. By checking early in the process, if you find something wrong with your records, you still have time to correct it.

It could be as simple as a wrong address or a wrong account, but it could be that even though you pay all your bills on time, a mobile provider or another company is showing that you missed some payments. It's possible to get errors corrected, but it will take time. That's why

Do it now!

Register with one credit company and get your credit score.

Any errors in your records?

you should start the process earlier, so your credit rating has improved by the time you need it most—when you arrange your mortgage.

If you don't have a credit history, now is the time to start it. You could be a very well organised person and manage your finances perfectly, but it won't do you any good if the bank can't see your credit history, and they will immediately put you into a high-risk group. You can start your credit history simply by applying for a credit card. It's possible just to keep it somewhere without using it if you prefer to use cash so you can manage your money better, but it would be advisable to make small purchases every month and pay the balance each time to build up a good credit reputation.

TIP: Always pay your credit balance in full, not just a minimum amount required by the credit card provider. Be especially careful at the beginning as it is very easy to miss the first payment. For that reason, it is a good idea to arrange the whole balance to be paid by Direct Debit from the very beginning.

As well as helping build up your credit history, paying for purchases with a credit card will give you better protection against losing money in many situations, for example when you are buying plane tickets or paying for holidays. Also, there are credit cards that give some cash back to you when you make purchases. The amount is only something like 1-3%, but why not get something additional?

REMEMBER: Keep an eye on your bank balance before the credit card payment is due to be taken. The last thing you want is not to have enough money in the bank to pay the Direct Debit, as that will have a negative impact on your credit score.

Lenders use automated impersonal credit checks, and, unfortunately, it's often easier for them to reject some people than to investigate problems further.

Credit scores are used by lending companies to predict future behaviour based on the past. All lenders have their own criteria, and your score could be different with each one. That means that just because you're not accepted by one company, it doesn't mean you will be rejected by another. But you do need to follow the rules to improve your credit score.

- Check your credit score regularly, especially before big purchases. It's also better to check records on all three agencies (Experian, Equifax and TransUnion), as different lenders use different credit agencies, and there's no guarantee that all records are identical.
- Have a credit card and always pay the balance in full. Short credit history won't give certainty to lenders, so it's better to apply for a credit card as early as possible and build your credit history over several years.
- Make sure that you pay all your bills on time and don't miss due dates.
- Fix any errors that come up in your records, and keep an eye on your records regularly.
- If you haven't done it yet, register for the electoral roll [8]. Don't forget to change your address there when you move so that banks can see your correct address later.
- If you are not eligible to vote in the UK, add proof of residency to your credit records. You can send the proof of residency (utility bills, driving licence, etc) to all three reference agencies and ask them to verify it.
- Check that all your recorded addresses are correct. It's very common to forget to change your address for all your accounts, like credit cards, mobile phone and many other places, especially if you no longer use them. Banks don't like anything unusual and can reject you if there are discrepancies in your records.

- Write to credit agencies and ask them to delink you from any ex-partner if you had joint finances. This will stop their credit history from affecting you. In the same way, a flatmate with a poor credit history can also affect you because they live at the same address, so it's a good idea to keep an eye on it.

- Unfortunately, things such as CCJs (County Court Judgments) for unpaid bills are wiped from your record only after six years, so if you had one, you need to wait for several years before you apply for a mortgage. But be positive: you'll have more time to prepare your savings, and you might manage more than 5% for the deposit, which will make your application easier.

- Applications like car insurance, mobiles, credit cards, only stay on your file for a year, so it would be better to avoid multiple applications for several months before your mortgage application to avoid the rejection.

- Don't reapply immediately after a rejection, but if rejection happens, do check your credit files for errors. It sometimes happens that a rejection happens not because of an error, but because of recent searches. So don't make too many applications in a short period of time.

- Paying insurance monthly instead of in full up front (for example, for a car) can affect your credit score. Not only do some insurance companies charge up to 40% extra for this, but it also can be recorded in your credit file. It's much better to pay in full up front.

- Before applying, it's always a good idea to check in advance if you comply with a company's criteria to avoid rejection, as that can leave an adverse mark on your record. If you don't meet their requirements, just don't apply to that lender.

- Do avoid multiple applications, which could be rejected and leave a bad footprint in your file, use eligibility calculators, something like MoneySavingExpert [9] have.

- Be consistent in your application forms. Fraud-scoring firms can spot inconsistencies, such as different addresses, different mobile numbers, inconsistent job titles and salaries. Inconsistencies can cause a problem, and you might be rejected without being given a reason, which will reduce your credit score.

- Paying your rent on time can boost your credit score. Tenants can register with schemes like Canopy [10] or CreditLadder [11]. Canopy is free and uses open banking to verify payments, reporting the information to Equifax and Experian. CreditLadder is free to report to one of the agencies, but they can charge £5–£8 for reporting to all agencies.

- Avoid credit repair companies, as not all of them use completely legal procedures. If you do need help, go to a non-profit debt-counselling agency, find more here [12].

- Cancel unused credit and store cards. Too many of them and too much available credit could harm you as well; keep enough to grow and maintain a good credit rating, and just cancel what you don't need.

- If you're trying to get a quote for a loan, ask the lender to do it as a 'quotation search' not a 'credit search'. This means that although the inquiry will appear on your credit report, only you will be able to see it, so it won't affect your credit score.

- Never withdraw cash from your credit card – this is a big red flag for mortgage lenders, and they might reject you.
- **NEVER EVER** take out a payday loan. Many mortgage lenders openly say that they reject people who take out payday loans. Using them shows that you can't manage your finances, and it implies there's a risk that you will fail to pay the monthly mortgage payments. Just stay away.

The good news is that even if there's something wrong with your credit history, it will be 'forgotten' after some time. Just start checking it as soon as you start thinking about buying so you have all the information.

Most banks will look back at 3 years of your credit history. So even if you have something negative in your file now, after 3 years it will no longer be relevant. Just use this time to prepare a bigger deposit, increase your salary and improve your credit rating—it's still only 3 years, not 20!

The Impact of Student Loan

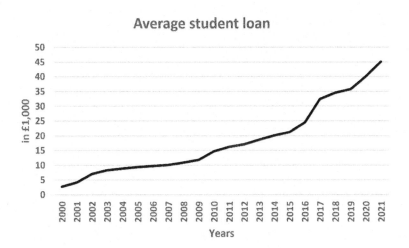

Source: Statista [12]

Figure 2: Average student loan debt on entry to repayment in the United Kingdom from 2000 to 2021

The vast majority of students graduating from universities have a student loan. The average student loan in England in 2021 was over £45,000, and it keeps growing, as you can see in the graph above. The good news is that, in terms of your credit history, student loans are not considered to be debt, and they will not affect your credit score. Yet, it will be part of your monthly payments, and banks will take them into account when they calculate the affordability of your loan, so you should take it into account too when you prepare your own budget.

There are complicated rules around when and how much you will pay toward your student loan, and you can check the rules on the government website [13]. If you receive your income through salary, your repayments will be calculated and deducted from your salary automatically. Check what interest you're paying on your student loan because if it's higher than the mortgage interest, it will be worth considering paying the student loan quicker after you have bought your first property, if you have some spare funds. You can pay it any time and without penalties.

Step 3: Mortgages

Step 3: Mortgages

"Some people want it to happen, some wish it would happen, others make it happen."

Michael Jordan

What is a mortgage? A mortgage is a loan that people borrow from a bank or another financial institution and that is secured against a property. If something goes wrong with the loan and the person can't pay the monthly payments, the bank can take the property and sell it to recoup the money. In this way, the risk for the lender is smaller for mortgages than for unsecured loans, so interest rates are much lower.

The bigger the deposit you have, the better the interest rates you can find. Banks consider that if you are willing to put 20% or even 30% of your own money toward the cost of the house, then the risk for them is lower. They are then willing to give you a loan with a lower interest rate. In Appendix 5 you can check the interest rates on some mortgage products that were available on the market at the time of writing this book.

The financial crash in 2007–08 was caused mostly by the mishandling of mortgages by banks in the US and other countries. Before that there were mortgage products with 100% LTV (Loan To Value), meaning that people could buy properties without providing any of their own money. It was nice – you just went, made an offer for a property, prepared some documents (much fewer than these days) and after several weeks, you had a house. But with the availability of such easy money, many people didn't plan their finances properly; they couldn't pay their mortgages, and the house market crashed together with the whole financial system.

There are very few mortgage products with 100% LTV now, all of them guarantor mortgages, and the banks usually require at least 5% as a deposit. During the turbulent year 2020, many lenders withdrew products with 95% LTV. But since then, many have returned, and now there are several available; as the economic situation improves, many more will come back.

There is also government help available for first-time buyers in the UK, which is worth considering before making the decision about your mortgage.

Government Help-to-Buy Schemes

There are several government-backed schemes that aim to provide help for first-time buyers to step onto the property ladder and to help existing homeowners move to the next step.

The situation keeps changing, though, and almost every year the government introduces something new or changes existing schemes. So it's a good idea to keep an eye on these government websites about available government schemes [14] and [15].

Do it now!

Check if government schemes are good for you

At the time of writing this book, the following schemes were available for property buyers in the UK:

- Help to buy: Equity Loan – for first-time buyers, only for new-build homes.
- Mortgage Guarantee Scheme – available both to first-time buyers and existing homeowners, and it's not restricted to new builds only.
- Shared Ownership Scheme.
- Right to buy.
- Help to buy ISA – not available for new applicants at the moment, but it still works for people who took them out before 2019.

1. Help to Buy: Equity Loan

This is a new scheme, launched on 1 April 2021 and running until March 2023. The government will lend buyers up to 20% of the value of the property, or up to 40% in London.

There are some restrictions on how it works:

- The scheme is for first-time buyers only.
- You can buy only a new-build home from a Help to Buy registered homebuilder.
- There are regional limits for the purchase price from £186,100 in the North East to £600,000 in London. See Table 7 for more details.

Table 7: Regional purchase prices for Help to Buy: Equity Loans

Region	Full property
East	£407,400
East Midlands	£261,900
London	£600,000
North East	£186,100
North West	£224,400
South East	£437,600
South West	£349,000
West Midlands	£255,600
Yorkshire and The Humber	£228,100

Source: gov.uk

- You have to apply for the scheme through a regional agent, authorised by the government, who will assess your eligibility.

How it works:

- Reserve a new property with a builder.
- Apply for a 75 % Loan-To-Value repayment mortgage (or 55% in London) via a mortgage broker or directly with a bank. Only participating banks are allowed, but many big banks such as Santander, Barclays, NatWest and Halifax do participate in the scheme.
- You still need at least 5% for the deposit.
- Apply for the government 20% loan with a registered agent (or up to 40% in London).
- The agent conducts all checks and authorises the applicant to proceed with the paperwork to complete the purchase.
- After the purchase, details of the government loan are passed to the equity loan administrator.
- You don't have to pay interest on the government loan for 5 years, and in the 6th year the interest will be 1.75%.
- The interest rate will increase every year starting from April 2022 by adding the CPI (Consumer Price Index) rate plus 2%.
- You have to pay off the government loan when you pay off your mortgage or sell your house.
- When you sell your house, you'll pay the equity loan percentage of the market value or the agreed sale price, whichever is higher.

Pros	Cons
• You can buy a nice new home	• You're not allowed to sub-let your home.
• 5 years of interest-free government loan, and a relatively cheap 6th year.	• Available only to first-time buyers, so if your partner currently has another home or had one before, you will not qualify.
• Could be cheaper than renting.	• You can only use it for new-build homes.
• Pay only a 5% deposit	• New-build homes can be overpriced, which will considerably reduce capital growth later.
	• You can only take the mortgage from certain lenders.
	• The amount you owe on the government loan goes up if your property value increases, and you will need to pay back more.

2. Mortgage Guarantee Scheme

This scheme was announced in the 2021 budget and launched on 19 April 2021. It offers a government-backed guarantee until December 2022.

How it works:

- The government offers lenders a guarantee on 80% of the mortgage where the borrower has only made a 5% deposit.
- This can be used both by first-time buyers and existing homeowners who are looking to move and require a 95% LTV mortgage.
- The purchase price has to be £600,000 or less.

Pros	Cons
• There is a much greater choice of what you can buy.	• The mortgage interest rate could be higher
• You won't need to pay additional fees.	• The mortgages are available only from participating banks.
• It's not restricted to first-time buyers only.	• You have to satisfy certain eligibility criteria.
• It could be a much cheaper option.	• It can take longer to complete your purchase.
	• This option could be more expensive compared to a standard 95% LTV mortgage of a normal purchase.

3. Shared Ownership Scheme

This is for people who can't afford the mortgage on 100% of a home. It offers people the opportunity to buy a share of a home (between 10% and 75% of the home's value) and pay rent on the remaining share. Later, you can buy a bigger share when you can afford to.

The house is usually managed by a housing association, and the rent for the remaining share that doesn't belong to the buyer is paid to them.

You still need to pay a 5% deposit on your share.

The scheme is available for households earning less than £80,000, or £90,000 in London.

You can buy a newly built home or an existing shared ownership home through resale programs from housing associations. You will have to take out a mortgage to pay for your share of the home's purchase price. Shared Ownership homes are always leasehold.

This scheme is not restricted to first-time buyers only.

Pros	**Cons**
• It's easier to find the money to pay for only a share of a house, so it could be a practical option for buying your first house.	• New-build homes are often more expensive than those on the secondary market.
• It could still be much cheaper than renting.	• There are many restrictions on what you can do with your house.
• Most of the houses are new or were	• You need to satisfy certain eligibility criteria, but the rules are not straightforward, and the housing association will decide if you meet their criteria.

built relatively re-
cently, so they
could be in better
condition.

- Eligibility criteria can vary
  according to local priori-
  ties.
- You will need a special
  type of mortgage, which
  is harder to find.
- It can take longer to complete your purchase.
- It could be much more
  difficult to sell it when
  you decide to move out.

4. Right to Buy

The Right to Buy scheme is available only to council and
housing association tenants in England to buy their home, but
there are good discounts available for those who qualify.

Houses	Flats
You get a 35% discount if you've been a public sector tenant for between 3 and 5 years.	You get a 50% discount if you've been a public sector tenant for between 3 and 5 years.
After 5 years, the discount goes up 1% for every extra year you've been a public sector tenant, up to a maximum of 70% or £84,600 across England and £112,800 in London boroughs (whichever is lower).	After 5 years, the discount goes up by 2% for each extra year you've been a public sector tenant, up to a maximum of 70% or £84,600 across England and £112,800 in London boroughs (whichever is lower).

Summary

The Right to Buy scheme could be a good route to owning your own house. Certainly, you need to apply and get into the queue to be able to move to a council house first, and then live there for several years before you can apply to buy your house. But there is a degree of certainty, and you can treat the house as yours.

When the time comes to buy this place, you will still need to arrange a mortgage. But on the upside, there are lenders who will treat your discount as a deposit, so, effectively, you will not need to save much for it.

As Help to Buy schemes come with several restrictions, whether you can take advantage of them or not will depend on your personal circumstances or your own preferences. It's a good idea to discuss these options with your mortgage adviser, as they have easy access to tools to consider different scenarios and advise you on what you can expect. Generally, there are a lot more houses on the secondary market than there are newly built properties that qualify for government schemes. Also, new-build properties tend to be much more expensive, as developers want their profit quickly. That means that the capital growth of a new house will be much lower for the first several years, and in a turbulent property market they can go down quicker and lower than other houses in the area.

How to Find a Mortgage Broker

When you decide that you're ready to start looking for your house, then it's time to meet a mortgage adviser to discuss your financing opportunities. You might decide later to take the mortgage directly from a bank, but meeting the adviser is usually free, and meeting them first will give you more understanding of what you need to look for. If you meet an adviser from the bank, they are restricted to their own products only, and they are required to sell them to you. So you will be better prepared if you already know what you need by that point.

A good independent mortgage adviser will have access to many different useful tools and market information, and they will be able to discuss your specific numbers and give personalised advice. Most lenders work through a network of mortgage advisers, and usually there is no big difference if you go to the bank directly. However, there are some lenders who prefer 'direct-only' mortgages. You can ask your adviser about them, and you can check their websites yourself to decide if it's worth talking to these banks.

There are advantages in taking a mortgage via a mortgage advisor:

- They will look at your situation and advise only the banks where you have a good chance of receiving the mortgage offer. The last thing you want is a rejection, as this will stay in your credit history records.
- Also, they provide useful help through all the stages, from preparing documents to completion, saving you a lot of time and stress.

- They are much easier to contact than banks, as in many big banks you only have access to them via contact centres without a personal contact. As a result, you might speak to different people every time who will not know much about your case.

If you Google it, you'll see that there are many places you can find a mortgage adviser. But as with many services, it might be better to ask friends and family for recommendations.

What to consider when choosing the adviser:

- Do they work with the whole market? Some mortgage brokers work only with a panel of specific lenders and promote their products. These could be good mortgages too, but, personally, I prefer to have information about all providers so I can compare. Just ask how this broker works.
- How are their fees paid? Brokers receive most of their fees from the lender. However, some do charge a fixed amount, usually after the sale completion, but do ask.
- What is included in their service? Will they help with preparing the documents and communicating with the lender on your behalf?
- Are they available outside regular office hours? There might be some situations where you need urgent help, and it considerably reduces your stress if you can receive replies quickly.

What Mortgage to Choose?

Most people know that they want the lowest interest rate possible, as this will affect their monthly payments, and eventually how much they pay to the bank (and which is lost the same way as rent). But there are many other parameters that will also affect the interest rate of the mortgage.

1. First is the amount of the deposit and what LTV mortgage you can get. Yes, you have only a certain amount of money. But you can buy a more expensive house with a 5% deposit and 95% LTV mortgage, or buy a cheaper house where you have enough for a 10% deposit and 90% LTV mortgage. In each scenario, interest rates will differ considerably. In Appendix 5 there are some examples of current rates on the market at the time of writing. You also can look online; there are several useful comparison sites to choose from [14], [15], [16] and others. These tools can be particularly useful as you can input your own figures and see the cost of your mortgage for a particular house.

REMEMBER: Some sites don't show information about the whole market, you need to investigate further by going directly to lenders' websites and talking to a mortgage broker.

When considering different mortgages, you will need to choose between a fixed-rate mortgage vs a variable rate. You can find details about different types of mortgages in the Glossary in Appendix 7.

2. Interest rates are different for fixed and tracker mortgages, reflecting what the market (and the bank)

expect to happen: will the base rate and other interest rates go up or down? Historically we have a very low base rate in the UK. It's expected to increase soon, and it will affect mortgage rates as well. If it's expected that the base rate will go up soon, many banks will start increasing their fixed rates now to reflect that in 2 or 5 years' time the interest rates will be higher. Tracker rates might stay lower for some time, but they, too, will go up when the base rate increases.

3. Often, there are similar products that have different mortgage arrangement fees and different rates. The higher the mortgage arrangement fee, the lower interest. The mortgage arrangement fee is added to the loan in most cases, so it's not a big difference in terms of the cash required, but the interest rate will be different. What should you choose? This is a number game, and there is no simple answer, as it depends on the house price. You can calculate the total interest + fee during the fixed-term period for different options and compare, or the mortgage adviser can do this for you.

4. If you want to take advantage of low rates now and fix it for some time, then for how long? Interest rates are different for 2-year fixed-rate and 5-year fixed-rate mortgages. There are also some 10-year deals available and even longer. What would be best for you will depend on your circumstances. Fixed-rate mortgages come with a penalty, called ERC (Early Repayment Charges), if you choose to repay the

mortgage earlier than the full term. The longer the fixed period you get, the higher the penalty; see typical penalties in Table 8. If you plan to stay in the same house for 10 years, you can fix the mortgage for that long. On the other hand, if you think you might want to change your job and location in 5 years, you might want to consider a shorter fixed period.

Table 8: Early Repayment Charges for fixed-rate periods

Year	2-year period	3-year period	5-year period	10-year period
1	3%	3%	6%	6%
2	1%	2%	5%	6%
3		1%	4%	6%
4			3%	6%
5			2%	6%
6				5%
7				4%
8				3%
9				2%
10				1%

The penalty is usually paid on the outstanding mortgage balance, and it can vary, although most lenders allow to make a 10% overpayment

5. What mortgage term to choose? The mortgage term is the time when the repayment mortgage will be repaid. Historically, most people took mortgages for 25 years, but now there are products with 30- and 40-year repayment terms. Monthly mortgage payments are lower for 30 years than for 25 years, as the capital payment is spread over a longer period, but you will pay more interest, even with the same rate, as it will be longer. As you can see from Table 9, for a 40-year mortgage, the monthly repayments are not half of that of 20-year mortgage. This is because you will be paying more interest, and the higher the interest rate, the lower the reduction will be.

Table 9: Monthly mortgage payments for different mortgage terms

Mortgage rates	20 years	25 years	30 years	35 years	40 years	Reduction comparing 40 yeas to 20 years
2%	£506	£424	£370	£331	£303	60%
3%	£555	£474	£422	£385	£358	65%

TIP: When you consider the mortgage term, you might want to go for safer, longer options. You must pay your monthly amount, and if that puts pressure on you, you will find that every month could be stressful. If you take 30 years to repay instead of 25, your standard monthly payment will be lower. When you have some extra money, you can then apply it against your mortgage as an overpayment. Usually up to 10% overpayment is allowed, so you get the same result, but with much less stress. See Table 3 on page 28.

6. If you decide to use one of the government's help-to-buy schemes, there could be other constraints that make the situation even more complicated. That's one of the reasons why speaking to a mortgage adviser can help to make the calculations of different options quicker. Have a look at what houses are available now and discuss with the adviser what mortgages are available for you.

7. While comparing different options, pay attention to other fees. Some lenders provide property valuation for free, but some require payment for this; some require you to cover their legal fees, and some do it for

free. There are even some products with cash back! It all adds up.

8. Having a bigger deposit will reduce your monthly payments later, as the interest rates for lower LTV mortgages are also lower. You can see some examples of options currently on the market in Appendix 5.

9. Do find out and consider how much extra you can pay toward your mortgage without penalty. Usually banks allow you to pay up to 10% more toward the capital without charging you for it. Your salary might increase, or you might receive a bonus or some other additional cash that you can pay against your mortgage. Paying the mortgage quicker can considerably reduce the total amount of interest that you pay over the years. Overpaying a 3% mortgage for 25 years with just an extra £100 per month will save you over £15,000 in interest payments over the whole term. What's more, it will bring forward the date when you are mortgage-free considerably, as you can see in Table 3 on page 28.

Discuss with the mortgage adviser what type of mortgage could be more suitable for you. Because interest rates are very low now, many people want to fix their rate for some time, so fix-rate mortgages are very popular at the moment. Other types can bring some benefits, though, like greater flexibility or an opportunity to overpay more, which will be useful if you expect that you are going to have spare funds.

What Do Banks Require?

When considering giving a mortgage to someone, banks and loan companies will look first of all at the affordability of the monthly payments for you and your credit history. All banks have their own criteria, and they are not published, but an experienced mortgage adviser will know what each bank requires, so meeting a mortgage adviser can help to navigate between the different requirements.

The mortgage adviser will look at your specific situation and advise you about your options. Getting a mortgage isn't guaranteed because first-time buyers are considered more risky borrowers. So to increase your chances, you need to understand what the lenders will be looking for when they are considering whether to grant you the mortgage and how much.

1. Banks are keen to give loans to people to make their own profit, and of course they need buyers for their business, but they want to make sure that you are a responsible borrower who can manage your finances and will pay all the agreed amounts on time. Banks will check at least 3 years of your credit history to see patterns, and even a single missed payment of your mobile phone bill can give them a red flag. Make sure that you don't have missed Direct Debits on record because you didn't have enough money in your account, and always pay all credit card balances in full.

2. Banks will check your salary and take any other income into account. Do you earn enough money to pay the mortgage? There are certain affordability criteria,

and banks will not give you more than you can pay back in monthly payments. Different banks use different multiplier, but FCA (Financial Conduct Authority), who supervises banks, issued new rules after the financial market crash in 2007/08 restricting how much money banks can lend. If you're buying with a partner, your combined salaries will be considered. In addition, any non-regular income, like bonuses, could be taken into account, although not in full, as it's not certain how much you will receive in the future.

3. Banks also check fraud data. You might never have committed a fraud, but if someone has stolen your identity and committed fraud, this will be in your records.

4. Your regular monthly expenditure, regular debt payments like a student loan, utility bills, transport costs, grocery and leisure costs will all be checked by the bank. So, to show that you have enough money every month to pay your mortgage, it could be a good idea to spend less on clothes, expensive holidays and other discretional expenses during the several months before you apply for a mortgage. Let the bank see that you have plenty of cash left every month. Your habit of keeping records will be handy here, as you can show it to the lender.

5. AVOID payments to any gambling sites! Even small payments to lottery sites can raise questions from the bank.

6. Banks will ask about the source of your money for the deposit, and they will double-check what you tell them. In most cases it will be your savings, and the bank will check that the money was in your account for 3-6 months before you apply. For this reason, it's a good idea to gather the money in advance. Some banks have introduced restrictions on how much your mum and dad or anyone else can help you, but others will accept a full deposit from someone else. In this case, they will ask for a letter from your parents or other benefactor about the gift or the loan, whatever arrangements you have. This is another matter to discuss with the mortgage adviser to determine what would be the best way in your circumstances.

7. Stay away from overdrafts. Although it's a useful tool on some occasions, if you use a bank overdraft regularly, it illustrates that you are constantly short of money. Some lenders will not give you a mortgage if you used your overdraft in the last three months.

The tables in Step 1 give a very rough idea about potential mortgages, and consequently, which house you can buy. However, you'll have a more accurate estimate after talking to a mortgage adviser. Some banks will lend more to a good borrower, so it's your task to show them that you are a good one! Some lenders will also take into account any additional income you might have, for example, bonuses.

To get AIP (Agreement in Principle), you will need to submit the mortgage application as normal. The bank will assess your situation even before you find a house, and they will confirm how much they will lend you. This will provide certainty for you so you know what houses to look for, and it will show the agent that you are a serious buyer.

The documents you will need to provide for the mortgage application are as follows.

- Personal photo ID: passport or driving licence.
- Proof of address: utility bills, bank statements and HMRC letters are all acceptable, but most banks will not accept mobile phone bills.
- Proof of your income: payslips from your job for the last 3 months, and some will require a letter from your employer to confirm it.
- Bank statements for all your accounts for the last 3 months.
- If you have other sources of income, you will also need to provide information about them.
- Be prepared to answer questions about your current loans or other obligations and provide documents about them.

TIP: If you apply for a mortgage jointly with one or more other people, everyone involved will need to provide this information. You should note, though, that it's almost impossible to find a mortgage for four people; and even with 3 people you will not have a big choice of banks.

TIP: It could be easier to manage the paperwork if you use a mortgage adviser. You provide all these documents only once to the mortgage adviser, and he/she will use them to talk to several banks and prepare further applications.

TIP: Add some more money for the deposit, even an additional £100 over the top of the minimum will increase your chances of being accepted.

TIP: If you plan to have kids, you'd better start buying the house and applying for the mortgage before that. Kids are very expensive, and the bank will restrict how much they will lend you taking into account the additional cost of the baby. As a result, you might not be able to get the mortgage 4.5 times of your annual salary.

Self-Employed Options

People who are self-employed are usually aware that it is much more difficult to get a mortgage, as self-employed income is not as stable as a salary, and banks consider such borrowers more risky.

But it's not impossible. There are banks who specialise in providing such products and who are prepared to look at your personal circumstances. It might be easier to find such lenders via a mortgage advisor, as they have more information available to them.

You will have to prove your income not only for 3 months, but for a longer period, more like 3 years. They will ask for confirmation about submitted tax returns and taxes paid, and they will ask for bank accounts—both business and personal—for 3 years.

If you have a stable business that brings you good income, you just need to plan the purchase of your home and be ready when it comes to the mortgage application.

- Try to ask all your clients to pay via the bank, if you receive a lot of cash, you need to put the money into your bank account so you can demonstrate your income later.
- As a self-employed person, you might need a professional accountant to prepare your business accounts, and you can show these to the bank. The accountant's fee is tax deductible, so your overall loss is less than the amount you pay. Furthermore, the accountant can save you the money on taxes and give good advice to facilitate your mortgage application.
- Try to save for a higher deposit, as your chances of being approved will be much higher.
- You might need to show higher income than if you were employed, as most likely the bank will agree to lend you a lesser amount than if you were employed with the same income.
- If your partner has a job, it can help if you apply together.

TIP: If you're considering quitting your job to start a business, you might want to apply for the mortgage first, while you still have a job. After that you can go on to pursue your dream and become an entrepreneur. The first mortgage is the most difficult; later—even if you are self-employed—you will have a track record as a good borrower, and re-mortgaging can be easier. Just fix the first mortgage for some time to give you a longer period to develop your business before you need to remortgage.

Step 4: How to Find Your House

Step 4: How to Find Your House

"Luck is where opportunity meets preparation."

Seneca

Start Online so you Know the Area Well

This is the fun part, much more interesting and exciting.

Ideally, you have your deposit money and the mortgage offer ready, so you can successfully compete with other buyers like you, and you're ready to make an offer.

Although many people would not advise you to look for the property until you're completely ready with your finances to save time and potential disappointment, but I think that some online searches can prepare you and give you knowledge of your chosen area, what prices you can expect, so you're not fooled by too high prices for some houses. This is especially important if you don't live in the area and don't know much about it.

The location is an important factor in determining house prices, and doing a proper search of your location and prices in the area can save you tens of thousands of pounds, even hundreds of thousands in the long run. The importance of a good location is stressed everywhere online and on TV.

Certainly, you should aim to buy in the best possible location for your money. However, if buying in the best location means a long delay while you prepare your bigger deposit, I would advise you to look at other areas with more affordable prices and consider it as just your first step on the ladder. Your finances will be much better in the long-term if you start early.

The biggest property websites are Rightmove [17] and Zoopla [18]. There are also some newcomers who try to get to the market and offer something better, but their share of houses on sale is lower. For example, OnTheMarket [19] was started by a group of UK agents to fight the dominance of Rightmove and Zoopla, but it has much fewer monthly visits. It still could be useful in a fast-moving market, though, as it advertises properties 24 hours before main websites. If you have time to search all the resources, you might find something special on other websites; but to save time, I usually use the first two, especially for the initial screening.

Both Rightmore and Zoopla have a lot of information about trends, current prices and historic prices; and when it comes to buying, you'll be better off looking at all available information, as it can save you from a potentially big mistake.

You can search areas with specific criteria, like number of bedrooms, postcode or several postcodes. There are also tools to draw the search areas yourself on the map, including several post codes or their parts, which could be very useful in cities, where prices can differ considerably on neighbouring streets. It's useful to save your searches and subscribe for notifications to your email address when new houses come to the market. You can play with criteria and save several searches, for example adding one more bedroom. You never know, it sometimes happens that a 3-bedroom house comes up cheaper than a 2-bedroom, so why not look at this too? Also, put a slightly higher price than your maximum, as there is the potential of negotiating the price down.

When you first start searching in a new area, it can take several long hours to look at suitable houses currently on the market. Certainly, you don't want to do it all again next time to find the same houses, so if you subscribe to regular updates it will save you time.

Do it now!

Subscribe to receive notifications about new houses in your target area

Do it for both Rightmove and Zoopla; there will be overlaps, but there will also be different houses on each site, and you will want to know about all of them. Do the same on other websites, too, if you decide to use them.

What to Look for in an Area

* **Transport links**. Whether you're looking in a city or in the countryside, transport links are important so you know how you can get to work. Even if you don't use public transport, it could be important for the next buyers when it comes to selling, so look for the nearest buses, train stations or tube stations. Usually, houses within 15 minutes' walking distance from tube or train stations are more expensive, so if the prices are too high for you, look at a slightly farther distance and you might find something within your price range.

TIP: Check how busy trains are at rush hour. We all want to live closer to the centre of the city to shorten our commute to work, but if you can't get on the train or tube in the morning and need to wait for half an hour for the next train when you can get in, it will not help you to save time and it will add a lot of stress. Maybe one or two stops farther will make your life easier.

- **Safety.** Is it safe to return home later at night? Will you feel safe walking in the dark? You can Google crime statistics in your area or use websites like Police UK [23] or UKCrimeStats [24]. There are also companies that provide security systems in houses who have their own tools, like ADT has [25]. There are some other useful websites in Appendix 6. As you get closer to your decision about buying, it's worth visiting the area in the evening to check how it feels.

- **Regeneration plans**. Major developments can affect future prices in the area, for example, high-speed railways like HS2 or popular shops increase the prices. You can find information about planned new developments on the government website [20] or on the local council website.

- **Mobile phone reception and broadband speed**. In the modern world, we can't live without technology, especially if your work requires you to have a good connection. Check your mobile phone when you view the property to see if there are problems. You can find useful information about this on the Ofcom [21] or Uswitch [22] websites.

- **Flood risks.** If floods happened in the past, this can affect insurance, and in some areas it could be almost impossible to find an insurer for your home. Your solicitors will order a report when they do local searches, but it doesn't make sense to waste time and be disappointed later, so you're better off checking the flood map for the area yourself [23].

- **Schools in the area.** Houses in the catchment area of good schools tend to be more expensive, and even if schools are not relevant to you now, this will affect future prices and how easily you will be able to sell, so it's worth checking school performance on another government website [24].
- **Other things to check:**
  - ✓ Major roads nearby can create noise and pollution.
  - ✓ Close pubs or restaurants can create noise at night.
  - ✓ Electric pylons might put off buyers when you decide to sell, and they can affect the price.
  - ✓ Big factories or plants.
  - ✓ Airports.
  - ✓ Big hospitals.
  - ✓ Stadiums or music venues.
  - ✓ Large schools next door can create problems with traffic in the morning.
  - ✓ Are there green spaces? It could be especially important for flats without their own gardens.
  - ✓ Are there sport facilities, and what other local amenities are available?

Check the information available online and plan some additional time to check the surrounding area when you go to viewings.

How to Compare and What to Choose

You might find some houses that have some potential for you.  I usually save them in a spreadsheet and include additional information for easier comparison. You can download it for free from:

https://buyfirsthome.co.uk/FreeGifts/

The information to compare: location, street or postcode, number of bedrooms, size of the kitchen and if it's separate, size of bedrooms, total square footage, price per square metre. The last one is a very important number, and usually agents don't publish it, so you will need to calculate it yourself. You can do that by dividing the asking price by the total square meters of the property, which also is not always displayed. If you need to find out what it is, you can check the floor plan, ask the agent if it's available or try to see if the information was provided when the property was sold previously. The EPC report can have the total square footage of the property, and this report should be available from the agent, or you can download it from the government website [25] if you know the address.

If you can't find the information about the size of the particular property, you can try to estimate it by looking at similar properties on the same street or in the same building, or you can measure yourself when you go to the viewing.

In many countries the price per square metre is a very important indicator, and it's displayed when the property is sold, but in the UK traditionally agents don't provide it. I suspect that it varies considerably because of people trying to sell for a higher price. At any rate, you don't want to buy a box house for the price of a castle, so do pay attention to it.

Another important thing to consider is whether you're prepared to do any work on the house. Many young people don't have experience in building or refurbishment work, and they don't want to do any. Many want to just move in and live, which is one of the reasons why new-build houses have high demand. But if you're prepared to do at least something, the range of suitable houses could be much bigger, and you can save a lot of money. If you see a newly refurbished house, it means someone did the job recently. They want to get their money back, plus compensation for their time, plus some profit, so you will be paying for all this in addition to a fair price.

If you decide that you can buy a property that requires some work, you do need to plan it. Will you do something yourself? Will you need to employ a builder? How much will it cost? In my comparison spreadsheet there is a column for building work. Do try to estimate how much it will need and the cost because you will need it for comparison. If there is a similar house for a similar price, but which doesn't require work, why bother with this one, which does need work? Also, if you have a good estimate for the required work, you can use it in negotiating a price reduction.

Even though buying a new house can be more expensive, it also has an advantage in addition to saving time: a share of this higher price will be paid by the mortgage, so you'll need only 5% (or 10%) of this at the beginning. If you need an additional £10K for doing the work on the house, you will most likely need it in addition to your deposit money. That could be tricky, but if the house is in a living condition, you might be able to delay the refurbishment and do it when you have more money.

ATTENTION: Even if you decide that you can do the work on the house to improve it, some houses could be unsuitable because you will not be able to get a mortgage. Many lenders have their own criteria for houses, but here are some red flags for you:

- No kitchen or no bathroom (or not in working condition). Usually, these houses are sold to cash buyers, and there could be an indication about it in the property description.
- High-rise concrete buildings. Some lenders will not give you a mortgage for a flat in a concrete high-rise even if you already have an offer with them, so you should double-check. These flats can be more affordable, but you do need to find a mortgage for it, so discuss it with your mortgage broker, as he/she might know which banks will work with such buildings.
- Big structural defects. You might find this book useful: *Structural Building Defects* by Chris Jenner [26].
- Houses with cladding problems. It's almost impossible to find a lender for these houses, even though the government issued new rules in July 2021 trying to reduce the pressure. You can read more about cladding problems in a Which? article in [27] or just Google it.

Although all the above problems can be resolved, and it's even possible to arrange a bridging or development mortgage to buy a problematic house, but for your first purchase you don't want these problems; leave it to people with experience, and just remove such houses from your list.

Using a Buying Agent

Buying agents, who act on behalf of the buyer, mostly operate on the high end of the market and they don't operate in all areas, but their knowledge and legwork could be useful for busy people. Traditionally they charge an up-front fee, and if you buy one of their suggested houses, you will have to pay them a percentage of the house price. Some agents charge a percentage of the amount they saved for the buyer by negotiating a discount.

Buying agents know their market well, and they ensure that the buyer doesn't overpay. As a result, they can save you more money than they charge, and they save a lot of time. If you can find a buying agent who works in your area and who doesn't charge much up front, this could be a safe option to try.

Buying at Auctions

From time to time, you might see listed a property that will be sold at an auction. The description will include details of when and where it will be sold, and many of them can look attractive because of the price they are listed at.

Unfortunately, it's not that simple. The published price is a guide price, and the actual selling price could be considerably higher. The reserve price—the price to which the seller agrees to sell—isn't published, and it's not known. However, the guide price should be within 10% of the reserve, so it's a kind of indicator. Very often auction houses will put a very low guide price to attract more interest from buyers and stimulate bidding, which usually results in much higher sold prices. It's not unusual for people to get carried away with bidding and eventually pay an even higher price than they could achieve on the usual market.

There are many reasons why people sell properties at auctions, but a lot of these properties have problems, which makes it risky for first-time buyers without experience. Many people arrange a survey to check the property even before going to the auction, and if they're not successful with bidding, this will be just lost money.

When a bidder wins, this immediately becomes a binding contract and 10% of the purchase price must be paid at the auction and the rest of the process should be complete in 28 days.

Do you have a 10% deposit ready to be paid immediately?

If there are problems with the house and the buyer finds out about them later, it will be the buyer's responsibility to deal with them, and it could be costly.

What also adds to the complications is that the house must be paid in full within 28 days, which is a very tight timeframe. It's almost impossible to arrange a mortgage in such a short period, even for an experienced buyer. At auctions, people generally pay in cash or take a very expensive bridging mortgage.

Although there are many success stories of people buying houses at auctions, there are also horror stories, when they lose a lot of money, or even all their money.

Auctions are risky, and I wouldn't recommend them for first-time buyers.

Step 5: Viewings

Step 5: Viewings

"The first rule of negotiating is: always ask for a discount. It costs you nothing to ask!"

Robert Rolih, The Million Dollar Decision

So, you have found several potentially suitable properties on Rightmove or Zoopla, you're ready to view them and you need to contact the agencies. I usually prefer to see several in one day to save time on moving around. Also, when you see several in a relatively short time, you still remember details and it's easier to compare. But don't overdo it; if you see 10 properties in one day, it will all be mixed in your head, and by the time when you go home you won't remember clearly where you saw what.

I usually prepare 5–6 properties to view in one day. If there are not as many as that suitable for me, I would still try to add some more, even if some of them don't look especially attractive, especially at the beginning when I start researching the area. Some could be too expensive, or some with lower prices might not look appealing initially.

You want to get as much information as possible, and even if some houses might not look completely right, I would go and see them: you might be able to negotiate the price and it becomes within your reach, sometimes photos of properties are not great and in reality, the house is much better than you expect. Even if you do not like it after the viewing, it's still will give you the experience and information to compare, you will have a better understanding of local prices, and what you can actually get for your money. Certainly, it's better to talk to several estate agents during viewings as different people can add more information about the market and the area.

To arrange your day in the best way, look at the locations of your chosen properties on a map and try to plan your travel and your timing even before calling agencies. Plan at least 30 minutes for each viewing, or even more, because there could be occasions when the agent will have another house to show you that is similar to what you're booking. When you're clear about what works for you, start calling agencies and ask for your preferred time. If you book well in advance there could be a chance that they can give you the time that you want. However, if you book 2 or more weeks in advance, and the market moves very quickly in the area, it could be that someone makes an offer before your viewing, and you miss out. On the other hand, if you try to book for the next day, agents might not have slots suitable for you. Also, remember if there are tenants in the house, the agents need to give them 24 hours' notice.

Do it now!

List three houses you would like to see

After gaining some experience you will work out what works better for you; you even can try to see 1–2 properties after work on your way home—why not?

I would strongly advise you to write notes during the viewings and add them to your comparison table first thing when you get home, while you still remember. These notes could be very valuable after you see 20–30–50+ properties. It can happen!

Try to avoid group viewings. Agents can use these to save their own time, and they want to create competition between buyers so they can achieve a higher price. Not only is it very easy to overpay in this situation, but also you will not receive the full attention of the agent during the viewing, and you may not receive all the answers to your questions.

What to Look for During Viewings?

1. Look at the condition of the property to decide if it requires any work. It's easier with newly built/newly refurbished properties, as usually you don't expect structural defects after good building work. You should still be aware, however, that newly painted walls can conceal previous problems, like untreated or improperly treated mould, for example, or structural cracks on the walls. In a new-build block of flats you will most likely be shown a show apartment, nicely decorated by professional designers. Do check whether the apartment that you will be buying is the same size, and do visit it to make sure that all the work is done properly to avoid unpleasant surprises later.

2. If the initial advert doesn't include the floor plan, it's a good idea to prepare your own, at least a sketch, preferably with measurements. Invest £25-£30 on a laser measuring tool; it will be very handy in many situations.

3. First of all, you need to make sure that there are no structural problems. For this, a structural survey later can give you more peace of mind, but it would be very costly and time-consuming if you order the survey for

every property you visit. A few ways you can detect some problems are explained by Chris Jenner in his book *Structural Building Defects* [26].

4. Go earlier and try to inspect the roof. Are any tiles missing? Is the ridgeline horizontal? If it's raining, check if the gutters are blocked and leaking. If water runs against a wall, it can cause damp in the house.

5. Look for signs of damp: dark stains on walls, peeling wallpaper, dark mould on window frames, a damp smell—all these could be signs of a problem.

6. Are the bathrooms in good order? Bathrooms take time and money to update. Would you be willing to live with this bathroom? Open the taps and check the water pressure.

7. Are all the windows double-glazed? How old are they? If they're new, the seller should have information about when they were installed.

8. Is there room to expand? Can you add value?

9. If you're viewing a flat, also check communal areas. Are they clean and kept in good order? Does the intercom system work? Is there a noticeboard with useful information and contact details?

10. If you're visiting a house with a garden, look for Japanese knotweed. Google it in advance so you know what it looks like. Also check on maps to see whether there are cases around the property, for example on Horticulture Magazine website [30]. Even if there is no sign of it, do ask the person conducting the viewing. They might not know, so ask them to check and confirm by email. They can't lie, as this would be

breaking the law. For Japanese knotweed and other invasive plants you also can check PlantTracker Project results [31].

REMEMBER: The bank can refuse to give you a mortgage if there is Japanese knotweed around, as this plant can be dangerous for the structure of the house.

11. Check what is outside of the property. Is it a noisy street? Are there pubs or restaurants nearby, which could create problems at night?

TIP: If you shortlist the property as potentially suitable for buying, it's worth going several times during different times of the day, as some areas could be busier and noisier at certain hours.

Questions to Ask the Agent During the Viewing

1. Who is selling the property and why?
2. Is anybody living there at the moment?
3. Have there been any offers? When? It could be that the vendor received a much lower offer a long time ago and none since, so he might now regret not accepting it. So there could be a chance that he accepts your offer, even if it's not much better.
4. How many viewings have there been of the property? If there were not many viewings, it could mean that the property is overpriced and there is a chance that a lower offer might be accepted.

5. If the owner(s) live there, do they plan to buy another place? Have they already found it? There could be a chain where several houses need to move at the same time, and you, as a first-time buyer, could be very valuable as you don't have a place to sell. Unfortunately, long chains mean delays, and if there are problems within the chain, the whole deal could collapse.

6. If there are tenants living in the property, ask if notice has been already given and when they are due to leave.

7. Does the owner need to sell it quickly? When would they like to sell? If they do intend to sell quickly, you might have an advantage, as you don't have a chain. If you already have a mortgage offer, you can arrange everything quickly, so potentially you can be a very good buyer and take advantage of that fact to negotiate a better price. If the market is slow, your discount could be considerable.

8. Is the vendor flexible on price? Would they be willing to accept a lower price? Nobody will tell you how much they will accept, but look at the agent's reaction, and you can make some assumptions. If the market is hot, and there is a long queue of buyers, it could be possible for the seller to achieve a price even a higher than the asking price, and some agents are very good at creating competition between buyers. If you have limited funds, you had better make sure that you don't get involved in a price war. Gather as much information as possible and have a good understanding of prices in the area to avoid that. I have met people who

bought at the top price who were struggling to sell later when the market calmed down. They had to sell well below the price they paid, losing a lot of their money. You are reading this book to avoid that happening to you!

9. What will be sold with the property? Very often people leave behind some white goods, like the fridge, washing machine or dishwasher. People sometimes leave some furniture, and it's useful to know about it.

10. When was the refurbishment done last? Look at how many sockets are in each room; old properties don't have as many as we use now. Are there enough for your needs?

11. When were the pipes and electrics last updated?

12. What kind of heating is in the house? Gas heating is cheaper than the various electric heaters; electric heaters could mean bigger monthly bills.

13. Check what the boiler is and how old it is. Quite often boilers work for more than 20 years, but they are not as efficient, and you can expect an old boiler to break sometime soon. Changing the boiler can be expensive, but this could be your negotiating point.

14. How old is the kitchen? You might estimate from looking at the design, but it's worth asking.

15. Check the sizes of the bedrooms, especially the smallest one. Regulations are changing, and what is considered a bedroom now might not count as a bedroom when you decide to sell in several years' time. You buy, for example, a 3-bedroom property, but if

one of the bedrooms is too small, you might find yourself selling a 2-bedroom house, so the price can go down. I saw houses on the market with bedrooms of about 4 square metres, which is a lot below regulatory requirement. Be aware that currently all bedrooms must be at least 6.5 square metres.

16. Was there work done on the house? Did it have all the required permissions? Was the planning permission obtained, if required? Was the work signed off by the building control?

17. Are there any guarantees still available for the work previously done?

18. Ask for EPC (Energy Performance Certificate) and check how efficient the property is. Lower energy efficiency means higher bills later.

19. How much is the council tax? You do need to know, as this will be your monthly expense.

20. Are there parking restrictions?

21. It's common for new developments to sell with a 28-day completion, which is very tight for most people. Do ask the agent if the seller will require a time limit for the completion. Your pre-approved mortgage will make your life much easier in this case.

22. If it's a leasehold property, ask how many years of the unexpired lease are left. Generally, you need to know that most banks will not lend you money for a property with a short, unexpired lease. Prices go down very fast with leases below 80 years; and 55-60 years could be a limit to find a mortgage at all, so you should avoid properties with short leases.

23. Two more questions about leasehold properties: How much is the ground rent? And how much are service charges? You do need to know how much you will be paying later, and banks also will take it into account when they calculate your affordability.

Are there restrictions on pets? Some leasehold properties have this restriction in the lease, so there's no point in considering this house if you have a pet or are considering having one.

TIP: Don't hesitate to ask many questions, even if some might sound silly. You need to have a full understanding. Write all the answers in your spreadsheet; you will need all this information to compare and make your decision.

TIP: Give your feedback to the agent. The better they understand your needs, the more chance there will be that they can offer you something that will be suitable for you. But be polite; it's not their fault if there is something wrong with the property.

Estimating the House Value

I wouldn't make an offer for a property if I saw only 2-3 of them. Even if you liked your first one and you have the money for it, you are better off having several to compare. If there's nothing to compare, it's very easy to pay more than you should. Also it's more difficult to negotiate without understanding the real price of the property, which comes with knowledge of the area and what is on the market just now.

Look at similar properties to the one you're aiming for:

- Look at sold prices on the same street, and on nearby streets. This is the strongest indicator of real prices. This information is available on both Rightmove and Zoopla, and it's best to look at both of them, as the information they provide about properties differs. There is usually a 2-3 month delay before the information appears on websites. You also can find information about how the house was marketed before being sold, so you can see previous asking prices and compare the condition of the house to the one you're interested in.

- Land Registry also provides open information about sold prices [28], and it can appear here quicker after the sale is registered.

- Look at similar properties and pay attention to how house prices have changed over time on this street.

- For how much was this particular house sold last time? Knowing how the prices have changed since then, you can estimate the current value, although if major work was done in the house, this can also increase its value. Whatever happened to prices in the area, most sellers would be very reluctant to sell below the price they paid themselves to avoid losses, especially if they did some work on the house. So, for you, the price that they paid is the very bottom price you can get, unless the house prices dropped and the seller is very motivated and willing to have a loss so they can sell quickly.

- Also compare prices per square meter for your target house and other houses in the same area. You don't want to pay considerably more.

- Look at the current listings on Rightmove and Zoopla. By including and excluding properties that are under offer or sold STC (Subject to Contract), you can estimate what percentage of the whole listing is sold. A high number indicates a hot market when properties are sold quickly. If there are not many sold properties compared to unsold, it means the market is slow and you might have a chance to reduce your offer.
- Look at the houses under offer. Are they cheaper than your target house? Or the same? Certainly, you can't know what the offer is there, but the asking price is an indicator, at least to some extent, if other people are willing to pay something comparable.

How to Choose

Some properties will be just NO for you, it's easy. But what if you have several and need to decide which one? All your notes in the table will be valuable.

Make a shortlist of properties, which you like, and be clear about why you like them:

- ✓ Good price for you?
- ✓ Good location?
- ✓ Good size?
- ✓ Nice garden?
- ✓ You don't need to do any work on it?
- ✓ Potential for adding value in the future?

Properties will not be the same, and you need to decide what's most important for you. Will you be prepared to pay extra for something important? How much more?

TIP: If, after going to a viewing, you decide that a property is not suitable at all, you don't need to write much about it in your notes, but do record why it's not suitable so you don't waste time on it again.

TIP: However, if something looks attractive, copy the line to another page for shortlisting.

You might need to arrange a second viewing for your shortlisted properties. Now you have more experience, and you have something to compare, so you will look at them differently. There could be an opportunity for you to discuss your questions with the agent and maybe to get some idea about the vendor's expectations regarding the price.

Things to check during the second viewing:

- Check the water pressure by opening the taps in the bathroom and in the kitchen. If they are on different floors, is there a difference?
- Check where the boiler is and see if there's a sticker from the last service. When was it done? Ask.
- Check the number of plug sockets in each room. Is it enough for you? They didn't use many in old houses, but our modern life requires a lot more plugs for various things.
- Are there radiators in all the rooms? Any signs of leaks?
- Check that you can open all doors and windows easily.

Making an Offer

You found it! So, what offer do you make? Of course, all buyers want to buy for less, and all sellers want to sell for more, that's just the normal negotiating process.

Gather the information and try not to be over-excited. You need to gather as much information as possible about the house and the seller, you need to have a good understanding of the current market trends, and you need to show that you are a good buyer.

If you are a first-time buyer, you don't have a house to sell. The seller, therefore, doesn't have to wait for you to sell, and you can move with the buying quickly and with more certainty. Some sellers could be willing to accept a slightly lower offer from a better buyer, so make sure that you have your finances and the mortgage offer ready, and make sure that the agent and the seller know about it. Agents are paid for their work by the seller, but they receive their commission only after the completion of the sale. With 30% of offers not resulting in completion, the agent will likely be willing to help you to complete the purchase. I have met some very good, professional agents who put a lot of effort into helping with the process. Keep a good relationship with the agent, answer their enquiries quickly and value their time and effort —you might need their help later.

In the most likely scenario you will be buying via an agent, so you will have to make your offer to him/her. By that time, you will already have a good understanding of the current market conditions in the area, what other houses have sold for, and you will have made your choice.

As in all negotiations, it's important to understand your own position:

- How much are you prepared to pay for this house? What is the absolute maximum and what would be a good outcome for you?
- What advantages can you offer to the seller compared to other buyers? For example, you can demonstrate that you have the money ready, you have the mortgage offer in principle approved by a bank, you have a stable job and a good credit history, so there's a strong chance that the bank will approve your mortgage quickly. Unfortunately, this can be a big problem for many first-time buyers, but if you followed the advice in this book, you can be ahead of the queue.
- If something goes wrong with this house, do you have another backup option? If you can walk away from this deal, it strengthens your position. Unfortunately, this will not work so well in a fast-moving market with strong demand from buyers, but at least you have another option if you're not successful with the first one.

It's also good to understand the seller's position:

- How long was the house on the market? Even in a hot market, the average time from advertising to accepting the offer is over 1 month; in slow-moving market it could be well over 3 months. These are averages, so, what about this particular house?
- How many people came for viewings? How many had two viewings? These would be good questions to ask the agent during the second viewing.

- Is the seller in a chain? As a first-time buyer, you don't have a chain. Your position might be attractive, especially if a previous sale had collapsed and the whole chain is desperate to find another buyer.
- Are there circumstances that require the seller to sell quickly? People might be desperate to sell because of their personal situation; divorce, death or risk of repossession can push them to accept a lower price. Your preparedness can give a big advantage over other buyers, if there are any.
- Has the seller already reduced the price trying to sell quicker? If that has happened, you might be in a very strong position.

Taking into account your position and all information you know about the house and about the seller, you then guess how much the seller will accept. On some occasions—especially in a slow market and with a motivated seller—it's possible to achieve 25–30% discount, but in normal market conditions, discounts are more like 5–10%. In a hot market and in popular locations, houses are often sold for higher than the asking price. This is where the buying agent can help the most.

Some Tips

- So, look at all available information, look at your finances and decide how much you would like to offer and what's the maximum you can afford.

- When you first make an offer, it can be a good idea to offer slightly less than your desired price—who knows, they might accept it!
- If they reject your initial offer, ask the agent how much the seller wants. It's unlikely that they will give you the exact figure, but there could be an indicator of how close you are.
- Remind them again why they should sell to you: a good job, the money is ready, AIP (Agreement in Principle) received, no chain and whatever else you can think of.
- Make the next offer as a not round figure, like £163,550. This will show that you put a lot of thought into it, and you considered the price seriously.
- You also can indicate that this figure is your top amount, and it will really stretch you. If the vendor is willing to deal with you after your pitch promoting selling to you, they can accept your figure, even if it's lower than they wanted.
- When trying to meet your offers and asking prices, you do not need to meet in the middle, you still can offer much smaller increments aiming closer to your price, but it works only on a slower market and if there are not many other buyers around.

Don't lose your head, and try to avoid being pushed into a bidding war. Don't be disappointed, there will be other houses on the market. The last thing you want is to considerably overpay by buying the most expensive flat in the house, or the most expensive property on the street, and find later when the market calms down that your house is worth less and you can only sell with a big loss. Or, even worse, that you have negative equity and have to pay the bank more to get out of your mortgage.

It might be easier to discuss your offer with the agent, and it's better to do this in person, as you will see if your offer is close enough to the amount the seller can accept. In a slow-moving market you can offer below the asking price, and experienced agents will help to achieve the agreement with a good buyer. So, it's in your interest to build rapport with the agent and convince them that you will complete the purchase; agents will make their own guess if you are the one who will.

Some agencies use a tender; they ask several buyers to submit closed bids in writing at the same time, and the seller decides which offer they want to accept. Certainly, the highest bidder has a better chance, but it's not always the highest offer that wins, they will also try to estimate who is the less likely to give up and follow through to the very end.

Staying out of the Crowd Can Give an Unfair Advantage

- Remind them that you are a chain-free buyer.
- Remind them also that your deposit is ready, and you have received the mortgage offer in principle to speed up the process.
- Be polite and professional. Agents are always very busy, so it pays to return their calls and reply to their emails promptly. Don't waste other people's time, arrive at meetings on time or re-schedule.

115

- Explain that it's in your interests, too, to arrange the legal process quickly, and you are willing to fit the timing around the seller's needs.
- If you got a chance to meet the vendors, try to build a good rapport and assure them that you will take good care of the property. It's someone's home, and it will be your home too.

They accepted!

Step 6: Conveyancing – Legal Process

Step 6: Conveyancing – Legal Process

"it doesn't matter how slowly you go as long as you do not stop."

Confucius

So What's Next?

Your offer has been accepted, and it's a very important step, but there is no time to relax. You have several months ahead before it's done, and some periods can be stressful. There is a reason why so many people can't complete the purchase, even if the price was agreed; there's still a lot of work to do.

Legally in England, the house is not yours yet. It will become yours after the exchange of contracts. At that point the purchase becomes legally binding, even though you haven't paid all the money yet. Before you exchange contracts, both you and the seller can terminate the purchase. So there is a risk that you already have some expenses, but the seller decides not to sell to you. It does happen when someone else offers a higher price and the seller accepts their offer. It's not very ethical, but it does happen, and the seller doesn't have an obligation to reimburse your expenses. However, you can still try to negotiate and get at least something back.

The same applies to you: you have the right to cancel at any point before the exchange of contracts, for example, if the survey reveals big problems with the house, or your solicitors find problems with the legal title.

After the offer is accepted, do ask the agent to remove the house from the market to avoid the risk of losing the house.

The agent should prepare a Memorandum of Sale, a document that confirms that the offer has been accepted by both sides. It includes information about the property address, price and the names of the seller(s) and buyer(s) as well as contact details of their solicitors. By that point, you need to choose your solicitor so the agent can send them the Memorandum of Sale to start the legal process. This is a useful document, and if your agent hasn't sent it to you, ask about it.

Contact your solicitors and tell them that your offer has been accepted so they start preparing the required documents.

You also have to contact your mortgage broker, or your bank if you applied directly, and tell them that your offer has been accepted. It could be a good idea to check whether the market moved and you can get a better mortgage, why not try? You already have one offer, and there is nothing to lose.

The bank will be checking your documents and the house, so they will arrange the survey from their side to make sure that the house will give them adequate security for their money. This will be a very basic survey. Its purpose is only to make sure that the bank can get their money back if something goes wrong, but an experienced surveyor will note big problems and write them in the report. Generally speaking, if you don't pay for the report, the bank can refuse to show it to you, although many will give it to you if you ask.

If you have any doubts about the property, it is strongly advisable to order your own survey. It can give the peace of mind that your house has a solid structure, and if there are some hidden problems that will cost you money to fix, you might go back to the vendor and discuss the price again. Unfortunately, the seller doesn't have the obligation to tell you everything about the property, but it's in your interest to find out, and it's better to do it early, before you spend much money in the process. It would be silly to find out that the house has structural problems or that the roof might collapse soon only after you move in.

There are different types of surveys with prices between £300 + VAT for a homebuyer report to over £1,000 + VAT for a full structural survey. Although the bank will conduct its own survey, their purpose is only to confirm that the property is worth the price, so it's unlikely this survey will give much detail. If you are buying an old property that is in a poor state, a full structural survey might be necessary.

As usual, it's best to ask for recommendations and read reviews, but also make sure that the surveyor is chartered and registered with RICS (Royal Institution of Chartered Surveyors), you can find a surveyor here [29].

Because new-builds come with a 10-year guarantee, you might not need an expensive survey, but I would recommend getting professional help to prepare the snagging list.

After the building is finished, the buyer usually has an opportunity to check the property and tell the developer if they have found any defects or unfinished work that they want to be rectified before the completion. These defects are called 'snags'. A professional snagger with knowledge of the building industry can identify things that are not up to the current building regulations, and he will give you peace of mind that everything was done properly.

Unfortunately, the survey might reveal unexpected problems, some quite expensive to fix. Arrange a quotation for any required work; many builders will give you a quotation for free. You can also ask the agent to arrange the quotations, and if you're not happy with potential costs, try to negotiate a new price with the seller, or decide that you don't want this hassle with this house.

How to Find a Solicitor

The solicitor has a very important role. There could be errors, considerable delays, even lost money, if they don't do their job properly. Prices can differ for the legal work as well as the quality of work, so it is important to find the right solicitor.

Do it now!

Ask friends or colleagues about a solicitor

The legal profession is regulated by the Law Society [30] and the Council of Licensed Conveyancers [31], so these are good places to start. Ask around for recommendations and check reviews; the more checks you do, the better. This is not the time when you should just choose the cheapest, check reviews first.

All conveyancing work can be done remotely, by email or by post, so you don't necessarily have to choose someone local. The agent might recommend their solicitor, but from my experience, they can be more expensive. Also, I feel uncomfortable with how much of my information, even if not private, goes to the agent, so I always choose an independent solicitor.

The ultimate purpose of conveyancing is to transfer the legal title of the property from the vendor to the buyer. Usually, the conveyancing process takes 6-8 weeks, but it could be considerably longer, especially for leasehold properties where the solicitors will need to communicate with the freeholder as well. Your solicitor should act on your side and make sure that your purchase is good, that there are no problems and advise you if they find any complications.

What Solicitors Do

- Check IDs and addresses of both the seller and the buyer to make sure there is no money laundering and no fraud from either side. The last thing you want is to find out later that the house didn't belong to the seller and it was all a fraud! You might have already seen such horror stories or read about 'stolen' houses in a BBC article here [32].
- Do property searches:
  - ✓ Searches from the local council, which will include information about the property and the area and any planned developments that might affect the property.
  - ✓ Environmental searches, including flood risk, contaminated land, risk of subsidence and information about waste sites close by.
  - ✓ Water authority searches.
  - ✓ Additional searches specific to the location, for example, mining searches.

123

- Check the legal title.
- Check the lease and communicate with the freeholder. They will inform you if there are excessive ground rent, service charges or any other problems with the lease.
- If the property was altered in the past, solicitors will check that all the required documentation is in place, all permissions were obtained and building control has signed off all alterations. If the seller doesn't have all the required documents—which does sometimes happen—it's not the end of the world, but it will require more time for communicating with the authorities to get the necessary documents, so considerable delays are possible.
- If the seller can't obtain the documentation, or something is wrong with the legal title, solicitors can arrange indemnity insurance to cover the buyer for possible future legal problems. It's just a one-off insurance policy that's tied to the property, usually at expense of the vendor. It's their fault that they haven't arranged all documents, isn't it?
- Check and advise you regarding the Fittings and Contents Form, which is prepared by seller's side and includes the information about other things that will be included with the purchase, like boiler, lighting, or anything else that will be left in the house. Some sellers take everything, but some might leave white goods, furniture and other items. Some sellers will try to sell the things they don't want to take, and all this will require an agreement between the parties.

- Solicitors will check if there are guarantees for any previous building work. New-build property that is less than 10 years old should have guarantees.
- They will check if there are legal charges, right of way or any disputes that can affect the price of the property.
- Communicate with the lender to check the mortgage offer and coordinate signing the mortgage documents.
- Negotiate and review the contracts to transfer ownership.
- They will send you the Title Plan to check and sign. You should make sure that it refers to the property you are buying and that the boundaries match what you expect. If you think there is any discrepancy, you should discuss it with your solicitor.
- Communicate with your lender to make sure that all money transfers are arranged on time.
- When the purchase is complete, they will register the title and the mortgage deeds with the Land Registry.
- Prepare the return and pay Stamp Duty, if required.

If you don't want delays in the process, answer all questions from all parties and send all signed documents back quickly. If you don't hear from your solicitor for some time, it's also a good idea to contact them and ask for an update. It might be a good idea if you set a specific deadline for the exchange of contracts day so all parties know the time frame; it doesn't give you a guarantee, but it can help all involved parties to plan their actions.

What Can Go Wrong?

- Difficulties with **obtaining the mortgage** for the house.
- The **mortgage valuation comes back lower** than the agreed price. Unfortunately, it happens more and more often as banks try to protect themselves and try to make sure that, if worse comes to worst, they will get all their money back.

What to do?

> - Go to another lender and try to get another valuation. You have not paid anything to the bank at this stage, so you can try another one. Ask the adviser which valuation company they use. Some big surveyors work for several banks, so there's no point in going to another bank using the same company. Even if the survey is done by a different person, he will see the result of the previous survey, and it's unlikely that he will give a higher valuation for the same house. I was in this situation before, and another bank did give the required valuation.

> - If you also feel that the price is too high, especially if another bank also gave a lower value, go back to the seller and try to renegotiate. You can use the valuations as proof that the price is too high. The seller can refuse, but the next buyer might have the same problem, and after several lost months the seller still needs to reduce the price.

    - If the difference is not big, can you find additional money to cover the difference? This only makes sense if you believe that the price is still good.

- **Problems revealed by the survey.** Although not often, such things do happen, which is why it's common to write that your "offer is subject to contract" when you negotiate the price. This means that the price can be renegotiated if new information is revealed. If the survey report comes up with some issues, try to find out if they can be fixed and how much it will cost you. If you have successfully renegotiated the purchase price, you will need to inform your lender, and if you've already received their mortgage offer, they might need to give you another one to sign. All this will cause delays.

- **Being gazumped**. This happens when the seller accepts an offer from someone else. Even if the property is taken off the market and agents can't arrange further viewings, people who saw it previously still can make a higher offer so that it becomes tempting to the seller. Try to fight, but if you can't do anything about it, at least ask them to cover all your expenses. The best way to avoid being gazumped is to prepare your finances and mortgage offer, be polite, efficient and fast moving. It's less likely that the vendor will decide to dump a good buyer.

- The **chain can collapse**. The more houses involved in the chain, the higher probability that it can happen.

TIP: If the seller hasn't found another place yet, or if the further chain is still uncertain, you might want to delay your survey and tell your solicitor to wait with searches until there is more certainty, so you don't waste money if the chain does collapse. One of the solutions to avoid it could be to agree with the vendors that they move into rented accommodation so that your part of the chain is complete—many people do it.

- The **sellers change their mind** and decide not to sell. It happened to us, and it was very disappointing, but we realised that it was our own fault as the legal process took much longer than it should have. It was a development project for us, and the seller had decided to do the same project himself. The delay gave him an opportunity to find additional money for the work, and we just lost a good deal. A lesson to learn here: prepare everything quickly, avoid delays from your side so you come to the exchange of contracts point quickly.

Unfortunately, not everything is under your control, but you can increase your chances of successful completion by communicating regularly with all parties and resolving problems quickly. It could be stressful at times, for example, you call your solicitor only to learn that they have been waiting for a couple of weeks for a reply from another side, so there has been no progress for a long time. Solicitors are busy, and they won't always chase the other side for replies. This is where you can help. If you have contact with the vendor directly, ask them to look into it. Most likely, they don't know what's going on between solicitors, but it's also in the best interests of the vendor to sell quickly. Alternatively, contact the agent and ask for help. Agents appreciate updates about the progress, and they also want a quick completion so that they can receive their commission.

I have a rule that if I don't hear from my solicitor for 3-4 days, I contact them and ask about the progress and offer help in chasing another party if they need it. It's better to make sure that the process is moving.

If the purchase falls through, it could be a very painful experience, especially if you have become emotionally attached to this house, and you might lose money too. Just have a break from it and then start searching again. This is another reason why it's good to have other options on your list. More properties are coming to the market all the time, and there is a good chance that you will find something even better.

TIP: Do read all documents. Mistakes happen, and if there's something you didn't agree or didn't expect—ask questions. Eventually, you will be signing important documents, and it's important for you to understand what you're signing.

TIP: When it comes to planning your money for the actual purchase of the house, don't plan it to the last penny, leave several spare hundred on top as an emergency budget. There are always some unexpected costs, and you don't want your whole purchase to collapse, and you lose the house you thought was already yours, just because you are short of £200. You could try to borrow from friends or relatives, but this could be embarrassing, and what if nobody has spare money when you need it most? If you have something left in your pocket after your move to the new house, believe me, you will be grateful that you have it.

Exchange-Completion

All checks are done, you jumped all the hurdles and resolved all the problems, mortgage offer has been received and the contracts are ready to sign. In most cases it will be an unimpressive 1–2-page document containing names and addresses, reference to the Standard Conditions of Sale, and it might include some additional clauses negotiated for this sale. It's important to sign the documents and send them back to your solicitor quickly to avoid delays.

At this stage, the solicitors and all parties will be discussing the date of exchange of contracts and the date of the completion. These dates could be especially important if there is a chain and many people are moving at the same time.

Although it's possible to have the exchange and the completion on the same day, it's easier to plan and arrange all the transfers if there is a gap between them, normally at least one week.

Normally a 10% deposit is required before the exchange of contracts, and your solicitor will advise you about it in advance. This deposit might be lower, for example, if you have only a 5% deposit and you're taking a 95% LTV loan. Once signed contracts are exchanged, the sale becomes legally binding, and you can lose the deposit if you pull out.

REMEMBER: You will need to transfer a considerable amount of money to your solicitor, so you will need to be very careful about the bank details. The solicitor will send you their bank details by post as part of their standard correspondence, but, unfortunately, fraudsters send emails with new bank details to lure you into transferring your money to their bank account. Be very careful; call the solicitor to double-check, and check 10 times before sending.

As a homeowner, you are liable for the insurance of your house, and the bank arranging the mortgage will require you to have the building insurance to cover major things. Generally, you need to cover your property from the day of exchange of contracts, as the last thing you want is for something to happen to the property the next day, and you end up having to meet huge costs yourself.

Banks often offer to supply the insurance, but in most cases, it will be more expensive than if you use an independent company. Insurance is very quick to arrange, you can do it the same day, but finding a better deal can take time. An insurance broker can save you time and money; ask your mortgage adviser, they might have someone in their team.

If you buy a leasehold apartment, insurance of the building is often arranged by the freeholder. It will be included in your regular service and maintenance payments, so leaseholders pay a share of it. Your solicitor would obtain a copy from the freeholder.

Do it now!

Write down what will you need to buy for your new home?

To cover your belongings inside the property that are not fixed, you will need contents insurance. Usually, contents insurance is not compulsory, and you should consider whether you want to arrange it.

Your solicitor will prepare a statement for your purchase specifying how much you will have to pay for legal fees, transfers, searches and Stamp Duty. You will be required to transfer the balance before the completion date. Normally everything is discussed in advance, so it shouldn't be a surprise for you.

TIP: The Standard Condition of Sale document—part of the contract for the purchase of the property— says that 'the buyer accepts the property in the physical state it is at the date of the contract unless the seller is building or converting it'. It would be a good idea to visit the property again and check that no disasters happened since your last visit. You can take the Fittings and Contents Form with you and make sure that everything is in place. If you're not happy with changes in the property, discuss with your solicitor how it can be resolved.

Once contracts have been signed and exchanged, the solicitors prepare the transfer of the title documents to be registered with the Land Registry, and they agree with the bank the date of the completion.

At the date of completion, the bank will transfer the mortgage money to your solicitor's account, and the same day, your solicitor transfers all the money to the seller's solicitor's account.

The solicitors finalise the completion documents and confirm the completion to you.

After the seller's solicitor has confirmed that they have received the money, the seller should vacate the property, if they haven't already done so, and the buyer can get the keys.

Done!

TIP: The completion day is a busy day for all parties, and several transfers need to be arranged. Often solicitors arrange all completions on Friday, and they might be busy with other clients as well. Don't expect everything in the morning; most likely it will be late afternoon, so plan to meet the agent to get the keys at that time.

Note: If something goes wrong, there could be a delay until the next working day, so have a backup option if you are planning to move the same day.

Step 7: You Get the Keys

Step 7: You Get the Keys

"Moving is an exciting and stressful transition that most people will go through at least a couple of times in their life. It can make you wonder if you're doing the right things and what the new life is going to look like."

Metropolis Moving website

This could be very exciting or very stressful. To avoid stress you need to plan everything properly, and there are particular points to pay attention to.

1. If you plan everything well, by that time you have given the notice to your landlord, if you were renting. Do check in your tenancy contract for how much notice you have to give your landlord. Depending on the type of your contract the notice period could be different: if you have a fixed-term contract, you can finish it on the last day of the contract, giving the notice in advance, unless you have a break clause or your landlord agrees to end your tenancy. After the fixed term agreement is finished, the contract becomes a rolling periodic contract. The minimum notice that tenants must give is 1 month if they pay the rent monthly. There is often confusion about what 1 month means. The notice should include a full 1-month rental period, so if your contract started on 15th, you need to give your notice on or before 15th to terminate your contract

from the 15th of the next month, and if you miss even 1 day, you might be liable to pay the rent for an extra month.

REMEMBER: Your landlord may have the legal right to deduct the money from your deposit for the whole month if the notice is not given correctly. It's always a good idea to have an amicable discussion with your landlord and check all the details in advance.

TIP: If you plan to buy your own place sometime soon, instead of renewing your fixed-term contract and signing another one, you might want to move to a rolling contract so you have more flexibility. It's much more difficult to finish a fixed-term contract earlier than it is to give notice to finish a rolling contract.

2. Take meter readings on your last day in your rented accommodation and notify your utility providers, water supplier, TV licencing, council and others that you are moving out. Most of them can usually be notified later, but telephone and broadband providers require 30-days' notice, so you need to plan it in advance.

3. In your new place you will have to do the reverse: register with utility suppliers (take meter readings), water, council and broadband provider. If your life can't run properly without broadband, you might want to arrange the engineer's visit in advance. Different providers have different time frames, so call them well in advance to check when they can come. I found that Virgin is the quickest, sometimes they can come almost the next day, but some you need to book a month in advance. If you don't want to be without the

Internet for a month, book in advance. You can change the date or cancel if there are delays with the completion.

4. Ideally, you want to have completion and moving to your new home the same day as your rental contract finishes to avoid paying rent and the mortgage at the same time, but this is extremely difficult to plan. Delays with purchases happen much more often than not. You don't want to find yourself without a roof over your head, urgently looking for a place for a short period. Even a couple of days could be complicated and expensive, so if you plan some overlap, your move could be less stressful.

5. Moving to the new place shouldn't be a big problem. There are removal companies who can do it at relatively short notice, but as usual, advance planning can save you stress and money. As soon as the solicitors start discussing planned dates for the exchange of contracts and completion, you will have more certainty and can plan your move.

TIP: You can save some money on boxes for packing your belongings by asking for empty boxes in local shops. They often need to pay for removing empty boxes, so they might be willing to give some to you. Using boxes twice is good for saving the planet!

6. It will take some time to unpack everything so you might need to have some things easily accessible:
   ✓ Toilet paper
   ✓ DIY tools
   ✓ Soap, toothbrush and toothpaste

139

- ✓ Towels
- ✓ Cleaning fluids, plenty of cloths, broom and mop
- ✓ Washing-up liquid
- ✓ Wet wipes
- ✓ Bin bags
- ✓ Some food
- ✓ Kettle, cups and coffee and/or tea
- ✓ Overnight bag
- ✓ Notebook and pen
- ✓ Chargers

7. If something is not right, you should take photos and contact your solicitor to discuss what can be done. If the vendor is in breach of contract, you might have a legal route to rectify it, but do consider whether it's worth your time and the wear on your nerves. When people move to rented accommodation, they expect it to be professionally cleaned. Unfortunately, sellers don't have such an obligation, so do expect that the place might be messy.

8. Things to ask the vendor before moving:
   - ✓ Ask to leave manuals for the boiler, thermostat and appliances.
   - ✓ Where is the stopcock for the water?
   - ✓ Reminder to leave keys for windows and all doors
   - ✓ Where are meters for gas and electricity?
   - ✓ Ask to leave any unused paint and tiles; who knows, you might need them.

9. Check if there are smoke and CO alarms. If not, install them as soon as possible. Battery-operated smoke alarms are cheap on Amazon, but they save money and lives.

10. Don't forget to update your address in all places, you can download the checklist from here: https://buyfirsthome.co.uk/Free-Gifts/ or just scan the QR code. Don't forget to change the address in Amazon. It happens all the time; you buy something quickly, and it goes to your old address.

11. Arrange the redirection of your post to the new address to avoid missing important letters for at least for three months, but a year would be even better. After some time, companies will start sending their statements, some do it only once a year, and you will see where you forgot to change the address.

12. Consider having mortgage payment protection insurance (MPPI). If you lose your job and can't pay the mortgage, the bank can take your house from you (repossession) and sell it. However good your planning is, hard events can happen in our lives. If you feel that you can't pay your mortgage, you should contact the bank and try to negotiate a new schedule of the payments. There is some government help, see [33], but they won't pay anything during the first 9 months, and they will cover only interest payments. One way to avoid repossession is to have enough savings so you can pay mortgage payments for some time, or you can arrange a MPPI. The usual advice is to have 3–6 months' salary in your savings in case something goes wrong in your life.

Table 10: Monthly house costs budget (a practical example)

	Monthly costs
The mortgage	820
Electricity	65
Gas	75
Water	46
Council tax	170
Broadband	30
Phone lines - may be irrelevant	20
TV licence	14
Building insurance	30
Content insurance	10
Repairs/redecoration	20
Ground rent - for leasehold properties	5
Service charges - for leasehold properties	100
Mortgage protection insurance *	20
Life and critical illness insurance *	20
Total	**1445**

* Mortgage protection insurance and life/critial illness insurance vary depending on the size of the mortgage and your age.

13. Plan your running costs after you become a home-owner. Banks look at your salary and your regular spending during the application, and they will not give you the mortgage if you can't afford to pay it, but you will need to have your own idea of how you will plan your finances. Don't plan everything down to the last pound; if you have money left, you can pay more to your mortgage, but if you're short, you will be in big

trouble. Do consider the possibility of a potential increase in interest rates, or some unexpected expenditure if something breaks
in the house.

TIP: Check with your council, you might be entitled to a 25% single-person discount if you live alone, see here [34].

14. To reduce pressure on your finances, you can consider having a lodger. At the time of writing there is a good tax break that allows you to have income of £7,500 per year from letting a room tax-free. You don't even need to report it to HMRC if you have less than that. You can find someone through the SpareRoom website [35], which is the biggest in this area in the UK, Gumtree [36], or Facebook [37]. You will be inviting someone into your home, so carefully check everything about the person. SpareRoom has good information to help landlords (you will be one if you let a room!).

TIP: Do check with your freeholder and your mortgage provider whether you are allowed to take a lodger.

Happily Ever After

Happily Ever After

"The world is round and the place which may seem like the end may also be the beginning."

Ivy Baker Priest

It wouldn't be right to ignore all the risks associated with buying and not to consider if buying your own home is right for you.

Life is generally risky; it wouldn't be possible to cross the road or drive a car if we concentrated only on risks. We know there are risks to our health, wellbeing and even our lives, but we learn how to avoid, or at least mitigate, them.

Buying a house is a very big commitment, and if you're not careful, many things can go wrong and cause significant financial losses.

What Could Go Wrong and How to Reduce the Risk?

- Buying in the wrong location because not enough research was conducted. Do check sold prices, crime statistics, flood area, plans for regeneration in the area or plans for closing a big plant or factory. If jobs are lost, the price of houses can go down, while new jobs will bring increased demand and increased prices. Floods can not only destroy the house, but there will also be problems with insurance, and prices will go down.

- Not having reserves for paying the mortgage. Even one missed mortgage payment can bring trouble later, and several missed payments can lead to losing your house, and definitely will result in a huge amount of stress.

- The property market can crash/decline, and the value of your house can decrease considerably. Generally, if you just live in the house, there's no massive risk, even if your equity in the house becomes negative, which can happen if the house is worth less than the mortgage. It can cause anxiety, but if you don't need to move, and if you just pay your monthly mortgage payments as usual, nothing will happen. Eventually, house prices in your area will recover. Problems could crop up if you need to move or if your fixed-rate mortgage period comes to an end and to avoid higher interest rates you want to re-mortgage, but new mortgage valuations could come in lower.

What to do:

1. If the initial fixed-rate mortgage period is fixed for a longer time—for 5 years or more—during this period you would have paid a considerable amount of equity and there will be less risk that the balance of the mortgage is lower than the house valuation.

2. Bigger deposits from the very beginning considerably reduce the risk of negative equity, which is why mortgage interest rates are lower for bigger deposits.

3. If you consider moving house, property market

corrections could be in your favour as you will be able to buy a bigger house for your money, even if you might lose something from your own house sale. If the whole market goes down 20%, a 20% reduction of a £100,000 house is £20,000, but 20% of £200,000 is £40,000, so you will be saving £20,000 if you move to a bigger house. That's why property market crashes are a good time to move up the property ladder.

- Something can happen with your specific house, for example, severe floods or hurricane destruction. How to mitigate: you need to be very careful when buying. Pay attention to flood reports, and try to avoid flood areas, and, certainly, you should have insurance covering all major risks. Also, discuss this with your solicitor during the conveyancing and read their report carefully. All these searches they do are intended exactly to mitigate these risks.
- When buying an apartment in a block of flats, specifically look for cladding problems. Unfortunately, after the fire in Grenfell Tower in London, many blocks of flats with similar cladding were considered unsafe, and they now require quite expensive remedial work. As a result, apartments in such houses have become unmortgageable and owners are not able to sell them – avoid!
- Buying a house is a very big commitment. It gives many benefits, but it comes with a great obligation. You will be responsible for keeping the house well and safe and for paying for repairs or replacements if something is broken. How to mitigate: make sure that

there are no hidden problems when you buy the house; ordering a survey can save a lot of trouble. Insurance can cover major repairs. Read the policy or discuss with the insurance company exactly what the policy covers.

- Monthly mortgage payments could be a burden, and if you lose your job and can't pay them, your house could be repossessed. You would lose your home as well as the money. How to avoid:

1. Have enough savings to cover 3-6 months' mortgage payments to survive the period until you find a new job.

2. Think about taking out mortgage payment insurance.

3. If worse comes to the worst, talk to your bank as early as possible to agree on a temporary schedule and a plan to repay arrears.

- Many older people remember that in the 80s and 90s the government kept high base rates to keep control over inflation, and mortgage interest rates reached 13-15% in some years. In the current economic environment, it's very unlikely that we will see mortgage rates like that again now, but what if...? Will you be able to pay your mortgage if the interest rate goes up? To avoid problems, it makes sense to fix the mortgage interest rate and keep it low for some time, which is why fixed-rate mortgage products have become the most popular now.

Buying a house together with a partner has a risk that your relationship can break down. If you're buying with a friend, the circumstances of either of you can change: one wants to stay where you are, the other wants to sell and move somewhere else. Life is life, and these things can happen, but what do you do? Discuss possible scenarios in advance and prepare an agreement in writing. Getting legal advice and a contract prepared by a solicitor would be even better, although it can cost you some money. Being aware of potential problems can prevent a lot of trouble later.

Financial Planning

Well done, you're already on the first step of your property ladder, but what's next?

Do you plan to stay in this house indefinitely? Not all people plan to change, but your family can grow, you might change your job and want to move to another location, you might want a better or bigger house. There are many reasons why people move to another house, and to get the most out of your next move, you need to plan it.

Do it now!

Plan your next five years: to move or not to move?

You might decide that it is time to sell and buy a bigger house. This is the usual way to move up (see the 3-Step Property Ladder Case Study in the earlier chapter "Why are People Buying" and in Appendix 4). As you need to sell and to buy at the same time, you will have a chain, which can bring more complications to the buying process.

To avoid this, you can try the following ideas:

- Find a first-time buyer for your old place. It worked for you, and there could be someone else wanting to start on their own property ladder.
- You can agree to a delayed completion date with your buyer. This could be a good option for all parties, as it gives more certainty. The buyer needs to finish his/her renting and arrange the move, and you will have more time to complete your buying and can plan everything.
- Try to find a buyer first. If the buying process is not ready by the time of the completion of your sale, you can move to temporary rented accommodation. Although it's not as simple, in this case you might need to store your furniture and most of your things elsewhere for a while.
- If your financial position allows it, you can buy a new house first, and then you will have more time and flexibility for selling your old place.

REMEMBER: You will need to pay an additional 3% Stamp Duty when you buy the second house, but you will have 3 years to sell your old place and claim this 3% back from HMRC.

- You can buy a new house and rent out your old place. Yes, there will be the additional 3% Stamp Duty to pay on your new purchase, but you will have extra monthly income as well. Also, you will have to change your residential mortgage to a BTL (Buy-To-Let) mortgage, but this shouldn't be a problem. Check on

Rightmove or Zoopla for letting prices in your area so you can calculate this option and make an informed decision.

If you don't feel like moving when your fixed-rate or discounted period comes to an end, you might need to consider re-mortgaging. Most standard rates applied by banks are much higher, so re-mortgaging could be a cheaper option. Start with contacting the same lender to discuss taking another of their products, as it will be quicker and there will be less paperwork. However, it also makes sense to shop around and see if you can find anything cheaper. Usually, getting the second mortgage is much easier, as you already have the history as a homeowner. Hopefully, your equity has increased, so you can also apply for a higher deposit and a lower LTV mortgage.

REMEMBER: You need to plan your future years the same way as you did when you were first buying. It doesn't make sense to fix the mortgage for 10 years if you plan to sell your new place after 2–3 years.

If you do want to stay in your current place, and you have accumulated additional savings and equity in the house, you can remortgage, take some equity from your house, and use it to purchase a BTL (Buy-To-Let) property so you have additional income. This is a very good way to build your wealth, but this is another story as it's a big subject of its own, and you might need to consult your financial adviser to avoid costly mistakes.

What Taxes Affect Properties?

Although the legislation in the UK is quite generous regarding residential houses, as opposed to BTL houses, you still might not be able to completely avoid taxes if you are a homeowner.

This is the list of current taxes affecting properties:

1. SDLT (Stamp Duty and Land Tax): Property buyers pay SDLT when they buy a house (see the tables in Appendix 1). Currently, first-time buyers don't pay SDLT for houses up to £300,000. Also, people don't pay SDLT when they sell one residential house and buy another one. But if you're buying the second property without selling the first one, you will be liable to pay SDTL plus additional 3%. You will have 3 years to sell your first house and claim this additional 3% back.

2. If, for some reason, you decide to let your house and receive rent, you will be liable for paying Income tax on the rental income. The legislation is quite complicated for BTL income, and you might need a consultation with an accountant who has experience with properties.

3. CGT (Capital Gain Tax): There is private property relief for residential houses, which means there is no CGT to pay if you just lived in the house and later sold it. But it can become more complicated if you let the house for some time and then sell it later. You will need to check your position regarding CGT with your accountant.

4. IHT (Inheritance Tax) At the moment, you don't have to pay inheritance tax on houses valued under £500,000 (or under £1,000,000 for a couple). Although it might look remote, if house prices continue to grow, your house can easily exceed the limit. This is something that is happening for older generations.

Chain of Actions

Chain of Actions

"That thread of ongoing action, that keeps you and me going, makes it easier to pick it up each day and pick up where we left off." Anne Groom, author of Value You

To avoid being overwhelmed by this big goal, concentrate on one specific action which will move you forward toward achieving it. You don't need to know everything from the very beginning; you will adjust your actions and find solutions.

What is the next physical action you can do right now toward your goal?

o   Record your expenditure
o   Prepare your budget
o   Open a saving account
o   Start regular savings
o   Register with credit score companies
o   Check your credit records
o   Apply for a credit card if you don't have one
o   Prepare your own action plan with deadlines for all actions
o   Talk to your mum and dad or your granny; if you go to them with your plan and show what steps you have already taken, they will probably be more willing to help, even if they don't have much of their own
o   Consider what actions you can take to find a supplementary income

- Look online for a suitable area and for suitable houses
- Find a mortgage adviser and arrange a meeting
- Apply for a mortgage in principle
- Prepare your table with suitable houses and conduct analyses
- Arrange viewings
- Prepare questions to ask during viewings
- See 10+ houses
- Write notes after each viewing
- Prepare the shortlist for your decision
- Learn more about the area(s) for all shortlisted houses
- Calculate the cash required and the monthly costs for shortlisted properties
- Prepare desktop valuation for all houses on your shortlist
- Arrange second viewings
- Make the decision: 1st choice (desired price – max price), 2nd choice (desired price – max price), 3rd choice (desired price – max price); the max price should reflect your resources as well as the level at which you will go to the next choice
- Make your offer and negotiate
- Find a solicitor
- Inform your mortgage adviser and your solicitor that the offer has been accepted so they start the process
- Arrange the survey or snagging list
- Prepare the documents for the mortgage application
- Prepare the documents for the solicitor
- Chase regular updates
- Sign the mortgage documents and send them back
- Sign the contract, title plan and other documents

o   Arrange another pre-exchange visit
o   Transfer the money to the solicitor
o   Contact the agent to arrange the key collection
o   Get these keys!

There is a logic in these small actions, and you can follow it. Where are you on your journey? You can start with any action that you feel is easier for you.

What other actions would you add? Tell me about them by email: book@buyfirsthome.co.uk, I will be very happy to hear about your plan.

Buying Your First House in 100 Words

1. Check and start building a credit history.
2. Review your spending pattern and how much you can save per month.
3. Start regular savings.
4. Find out how much you can borrow and how much deposit you will need.
5. Prepare your budget.
6. Meet a mortgage adviser and arrange a mortgage offer in principle.
7. Start looking online for your house.
8. Arrange viewings.
9. Short-list best options.
10. Compare options and make an offer.
11. Find a solicitor.
12. Instruct your solicitor and the mortgage broker to start the legal process.
13. Quickly prepare all required documents.
14. Get the keys and move.
15. If not successful – go to step 7.

Acknowledgements

I want to thank all the people who have helped me in writing this book.

First of all, I would like to thank Chris Payne; without him I would never have dared to start. His enthusiasm, inspiration and guidance helped me at every stage. I knew nothing about writing and publishing books, and he showed me the way to do it and how to stay focused. He showed me the path, and got me thinking, 'OK, maybe I can do it too'.

I want to thank Jennifer Simmons for her patience and her great help with editing this book, Ruhul Amin for help with illustrations and Mohamed Musthafa for designing the book cover.

I also want to thank all the other people, friends and family who had the patience to read my book and gave their thoughts on how to improve it.

Moving Forward

I hope that after reading this book you feel more confident about buying your own place and ready to start your journey. Prepare your plan and get started. Owning a property can bring huge benefits and stability in your life, and it will protect you in your old age.

If you enjoyed this book and found it useful, write a review to help other first-time buyers.

I would be happy to hear your thoughts about the book. Did you like it? What can be improved? Was anything unclear?

Was it of help to you? What can be added?

Drop me a line at book@buyfirsthome.co.uk with your questions, concerns or suggestions.

If you find that you still have questions or need help, please feel free to visit my website:

https://buyfirsthome.co.uk/

or book a free call:

https://buyfirsthome.co.uk/FreeCall/

Happy journey!

Appendix 1: Stamp Duty Land Tax

In the UK, Stamp Duty tax is payable by a buyer of the property at the time of purchase. There is some time to submit the information and transfer the money to HMRC, but usually, the solicitor collects whatever is due before the completion.

From the government website:

"If you're buying your first home

You can claim a discount (relief) if you buy your first home before 8 July 2020 or from 1 July 2021. This means you'll pay:

- no SDLT up to £300,000

- 5% SDLT on the portion from £300,001 to £500,000

You're eligible if you and anyone else you're buying with are first-time buyers.

If the price is over £500,000, you follow the rules for people who've bought a home before."

On the right are some examples of how much Stamp Duty you will pay for different house prices

House Price	SDLT
Up to £300,000	£0
£350,000	£2,500
£400,000	£5,000
£450,000	£7,500

For other purchases, the tax is calculated as follows:

Property or lease premium or transfer value	SDLT rate	Additional Property 3%
Up to £125,000	0%	3%*
The next £125,000 (the portion from £125,001 to £250,000)	2%	5%
The next £675,000 (the portion from £250,001 to £925,000)	5%	8%
The next £575,000 (the portion from £925,001 to £1.5 million)	10%	13%
The remaining amount (the portion above £1.5 million)	12%	15%

* An additional property purchased for less than £40k will attract 0% tax. For purchases from £40k to £125k the additional SDLT rate will be 3% on the full purchase price.

Appendix 2: Average Cost of Renting vs Buying by Region

Region	Monthly cost of owning	Monthly cost of renting	Monthly difference	Annual difference
London	£1,408	£1,791	£384	£4,608
South East	£1,018	£1,232	£215	£2,580
East Anglia	£739	£907	£168	£2,016
Scotland	£527	£683	£156	£1,872
South West	£1,018	£1,232	£153	£1,836
North West	£576	£723	£147	£1,764
Wales	£546	£665	£119	£1,428
West Midlands	£638	£756	£118	£1,416
North East	£484	£599	£115	£1,380
East Midlands	£632	£706	£75	£900
Yorkshire & The Humber	£557	£628	£72	£864
Northern Ireland	£445	£490	£45	£540

Source: https://www.which.co.uk/news/2021/04/is-it-cheaper-to-own-or-rent-a-home/

Appendix 3: Renting vs Buying

In most areas of the UK it's cheaper to pay a mortgage than to pay rent. Furthermore, it's much cheaper when you compare "lost money" on rent with "lost money" on interest payments because part of the mortgage payment goes against the capital repayment and it's still your money.

I took a couple of locations almost randomly and calculated what happens over 5 years if someone rents or buys. People can buy properties on the secondary market, or they can buy a new-build and take the opportunity of government support in the form of a loan of up to 40% in London, or up to 20% outside London.

	Three Boys Area 1 South West London			Three Girls Area 2 Outside London	
Renting 1 bedroom apartment	David			Jane	
Rent per month	£1,200			£525	
Rent paid over 5 years	£72,000			£31,500	
Buying a 1-bedroom apartment and taking the first mortgage 95% LTV, deposit required £15,000	Neil			Linda	
House price		£300,000			£100,000
Initial deposit year 1	£15,000			£5,000	
Mortgage 95% LTV	£285,000			£95,000	
Leek United Building Society 2-year fixed mortgage, 30 years' repayment period		2.37%			1.55%
Monthly mortgage payments	£1,108			£330	
Mortgage payments for 2 years	£26,592			£7,920	
Outstanding mortgage at the end of 2 years	£271,650			£89,946	
Equity paid	£13,350			£5,054	

Mortgage interest paid over 2 years	£13,242			£2,866	
Estimated equity left after 2 years of paying repayment mortgage, without taking into account possible growth in property value	£28,350			£10,054	

Usually it makes sense to remortgage at the end of the fixed-rate period to avoid higher interest rates charged by the bank after that; by adding just under £3K you can remortgage to a better 90% LTV mortgage

New mortgage 90% LTV; to avoid more complex calculations, we assume the value of the property is the same		£300,000			£100,000
Currently on the market there is a 3-year fixed 90% LTV mortgage from Nationwide					
Interest		1.99%			1.99%
Mortgage value	£270,000			£90,000	
Deposit for the second mortgage	£30,000			£10,000	
Monthly mortgage payments, which are now even less than for the previous mortgage, and much less than the rent payments	£997			£332	
Mortgage payments over 3-year fixed-rate period	£35,892			£11,952	

Actually, calculating savings, we need to compare rent with interest payments, as both are "lost money". The capital part of the mortgage stays with us, so it could be considered as sitting on another savings account (a mortgage account). This saving has some restrictions as people can't take them easily, but it's still your money, even without easy access.

Estimated interest paid during the second mortgage					
Outstanding mortgage at the end of 3 years	£249,662			£83,221	
Equity paid	£20,338			£6,779	
Mortgage interest paid over 3 years	£15,554			£5,173	
Estimated equity left after 2 years of paying repayment mortgage, without taking into account possible growth in property value	£50,338	<= capital		£16,779	<= capital
Total interest paid over 5 years	£28,796			£8,039	
Total savings over 5 years		43,204			£23,461

This savings figure will most likely be even higher as rent can go up, and renters will pay even more. House prices could increase as well, leaving house owners with even more equity because the mortgage you borrow from the bank doesn't go up when house prices go up!

Buying a 1-bedroom flat using the government loan scheme	Tom		Amanda	
House price of the new-buid will be higher	£400,000		£160,000	
Deposit required 5%	£20,000		£8,000	
Interest on 55%/75% LTV mortgage, Newbury BS 5-year fixed, repayment 30 years		1.69%		1.69%
Mortgage taken	£220,000		£120,000	
Government loan 40% or 20%, no interest to pay for 5 years	£160,000		£32,000	
Monthly payments (much less than monthly rent)	£779		£425	
Mortgage payments over 5 years	£46,740		£25,500	
Mortgage left at the end of 5 years	£190,605		£103,937	
Capital repaid	£29,395		£16,033	
Equity at the end of 5 years	£49,395	<= capital	£24,033	<= capital
Mortgage interest paid in 5 years (total mortgage paid minus the part that is related to capital)	£17,345		£9,457	
Total savings over 5 years		£54,655		£22,033

More options could be open with a bigger deposit, including paying back the government loan and taking a bank mortgage with higher deposit, or remortgaging for another period and keeping the initial government loan and paying the interest after year 6.

175

Appendix 4: 3-Step Property Ladder

This is a hypothetical example because we certainly can't predict future house prices and future interest rates, but the estimation is based on historic and current figures. The actual figures can be worse, but they can be better. The 5% annual growth used in this example will give the house additional value of only £162,900 for the first house after 10 years, but we know that in many areas house prices can double during a 10-year period.

Step 1	House 1 bought at the beginning of year 1	£100,000
Year 1	Deposit paid for house 1	£5,000
	Other costs	£2,000
	Total cash for buying house	£7,000
	Mortgage 95% LTV taken for house 1	£95,000
	Interest rate for the mortgage 95% LTV, fixed for 5 years, repayment 30 years	2.54%
	Monthly mortgage payment, including interest and capital repayment	£377

End of year 5	Mortgage payments over 5 years		£22,620
	Remaining mortgage at the end of year 5		£83,737
	Capital repaid over 5 years		£11,263
	Interest paid over 5 years		£11,357
	Assuming 5% annual growth in house prices, house 1 value at the end of year 5		£127,600
	Equity in the house, which can be used for the next purchase		£43,863
Step 2	Selling house 1 and using equity for paying the deposit for house 2		
	House 2 purchase price		**£170,000**
	Deposit paid for house 2		£42,500
	Mortgage 75% LTV taken for house 2		£127,500
	Interest rate for the mortgage 75% LTV, fixed for 5 years, repayment 30 years		1.69%
	Monthly mortgage payments are even smaller for more expensive house 2!		£452
End of year 10	Mortgage payments over 5 years		£27,120
	Mortgage left after 5 years		£110,465
	Capital repaid over 5 years		£17,035
	Interest paid over 5 years		£10,085
	Assuming 5% annual growth in house prices, house 2 value at the end of year 10		£216,967
	Equity in the house, which can be used for the next purchase		£106,502

Step 3	Selling house 2 and using equity for paying the deposit for house 3	
Start of year 11	House 3 purchase price	**£420,000**
	Deposit	£105,000
	Mortgage 75% LTV taken for house 3	£315,000
	Interest rate for the mortgage 75% LTV, fixed for 5 years, repayment 30 years. Interesting, for the same LTV mortgage, interest rate is lower for bigger and more expensive houses - banks trust more if people already have many years of monthly mortgage payments	1.80%
	Monthly mortgage payments	£1,132
End of year 15	Mortgage payments over 5 years	£67,920
	Mortgage left after 5 years	£273,534
	Capital repaid over 5 years	£41,466
	Interest paid over 5 years	£26,454
	Assuming 5% annual growth in house prices, house 3 value at the end of year 15	£536,038
	Equity in the house, which can be used for the next purchase	**£262,504**

Many options are available with the growth of equity: you can remortgage to reduce monthly payments, take part of equity as cash and use it for buying another house, use the cash for other purposes or buy a bigger house 4.

Appendix 5: Mortgage Rates

2-year mortgages for first-time buyers 95% LTV

Property value £100,000, Deposit £5,000,
Mortgage 95% LTV, Mortgage term 30 years, Repayment

Lender	Monthly payment	Initial rate	Product fees	Initial term cost	APRC
Progressive Building Society	£325	1.44%	£0	£7,803	4.30%
2 year discounted	for 24 months				
Progressive Building Society	£330	1.55%	£0	£7,924	4.30%
2 year fixed	for 24 months				
Newcastle Building Society	£368	2.35%	£999	£10,071	3.80%
2 year discounted	until 31/07/2024				
Leek United Building Society	£369	2.37%	£995	£9,871	5.10%
2 year fixed	until 31/05/2024				
Charley Building Society	£370	2.39%	£599	£9,628	5.00%
2 year discounted	for 24 months				
The Nottingham	£370	2.39%	£999	£9,903	4.10%
2 year fixed	until 31/03/2024				
Monmouthshire Building Society	£370	2.39%	£1,149	£10,223	4.60%
2 year fixed	for 24 months				
Newcastle Building Society	£373	2.45%	£1,198	£10,388	3.90%
2 year fixed	until 29/07/2024				

Source: https://www.moneysupermarket.com/mortgages/first-time-buyers/

5-year mortgages for first-time buyers 95% LTV

Property value £100,000, Deposit £5,000,
Mortgage 95% LTV, Mortgage term 30 years, Repayment

Lender	Monthly pay- ment	Initial rate	Prod- uct fees	Initial term cost	APRC
Skipton Building Society	£377	2.54%	£0	£22,646	4.10%
5 year fixed	until 31/08/2027				
Monmouthshire Building Society	£385	2.69%	£1,149	£24,433	4.20%
5 year fixed	for 60 months				
Leeds United Building Society	£390	2.80%	£999	£24,455	4.70%
5 year fixed	until 30/06/2027				
Principality Build- ing Society	£392	2.83%	£0	£23,520	4.00%
5 year fixed	until 30/06/2027				
The Cumberland	£392	2.83%	£999	£24,531	4.00%
5 year fixed	until 01/06/2027				
Clydesdale Bank	£392	2.83%	£999	£24,551	4.20%
5 year fixed	until 31/05/2027				
Newcastle Build- ing Society	£393	2.85%	£1,198	£25,011	3.70%
5 year fixed	until 31/07/2027				
Scottish Building Society	£395	2.89%	£995	£24,870	4.60%
5 year fixed	for 60 months				

Source: https://www.moneysupermarket.com/mortgages/first-time-
buyers/

182

2-year mortgages for first-time buyers 90% LTV

Property value £100,000, Deposit £10,000,
Mortgage 90% LTV, Mortgage term 30 years, Repayment

Lender	Monthly payment	Initial rate	Product fees	Initial term cost	APRC
Cumberland	£307	1.42%	£999	£8,361	4.20%
2 year discounted	for 24 months				
Progressive Building Society	£308	1.44%	£0	£7,392	4.30%
2 year discounted	for 24 months				
Progressive Building Society	£313	1.55%	£0	£7,506	4.30%
2 year fixed	for 24 months				
Yorkshire Building Society	£321	1.74%	£995	£8,701	4.10%
2 year tracker	until 30/04/2024				
Natwest	£324	1.80%	£995	£8,795	3.80%
2 year fixed	until 30/04/2024				
Royal Bank of Scotland	£324	1.80%	£995	£8,795	3.80%
2 year fixed	until 30/04/2024				
Newcastle Building Society	£3	1.80%	£999	£8,828	3.60%
2 year tracker	until 31/07/2024				
HSBC	£326	1.84%	£999	£8,828	3.60%
2 year tracker	for 24 months				

Source: https://www.moneysupermarket.com/mortgages/first-time-buyers/

5-year mortgages for first-time buyers 90% LTV

*Property value £100,000, Deposit £10,000,
Mortgage 90% LTV, Mortgage term 30 years, Repayment*

Lender	Monthly payment	Initial rate	Product fees	Initial term cost	APRC
Clydesdale Bank	£344	2.25%	£1,999	£22,680	4.10%
5 year fixed	until 31/05/2027				
Clydesdale Bank	£348	2.33%	£999	£22,026	4.00%
5 year fixed	until 31/05/2027				
HSBC	£348	2.33%	£999	£21,906	3.40%
5 year fixed	until 30/04/2027				
Charley Building Society	£349	2.35%	£675	£21,743	4.40%
5 year discounted	for 60 months				
Cumberland	£350	2.38%	£1,999	£23,020	4.00%
5 year fixed	until 1/06/2027				
first direct	£350	2.39%	£490	£21,519	3.40%
5 year fixed	for 60 months				
Natwest	£351	2.41%	£995	£22,110	3.60%
5 year fixed	until 30/04/2027				
Royal Bank of Scotland	£351	2.41%	£995	£22,110	3.60%
5 year fixed	until 30/04/2027				

Source: https://www.moneysupermarket.com/mortgages/first-time-buyers/

Appendix 6: References and Useful Resources

References

[1]   Statista, "Residential Real Estate," 2022. [Online]. Available: https://www.statista.com/statistics/557862/total-first-time-buyers-united-kingdom/.

[2]   Which?, "Mortgages & property," 2021. [Online]. Available: https://www.which.co.uk/news/2021/04/is-it-cheaper-to-own-or-rent-a-home/.

[3]   Zoopla, "Property Features," 2021. [Online]. Available: https://www.zoopla.co.uk/discover/featured-homes/top-10-most-affordable-places-to-live/.

[4]   R. Kiyosaki, Rich Dad Poor Dad: What the Rich Teach Their Kids About Money That the Poor and Middle Class Do Not!, 2017.

[5]   Experian, [Online]. Available: https://www.experian.co.uk/.

[6]   Equifax, [Online]. Available: https://www.equifax.co.uk/.

[7]   Transunion, [Online]. Available:
https://www.transunion.co.uk/.

[8]   gov.uk, "Register to vote," [Online]. Available:
https://www.gov.uk/register-to-vote.

[9]   Moneysavingexpert, [Online]. Available:
https://www.moneysavingexpert.com/.

[10]   InsureStreet Limited, [Online]. Available:
https://www.canopy.rent/.

[11]   CreditLadder, [Online]. Available:
https://www.creditladder.co.uk/.

[12]   Statista, "Education & Science," 2022. [Online].
Available:
https://www.statista.com/statistics/376423/uk-
student-loan-debt/.

[13]   gov.uk, "Repaying your student loan," [Online].
Available: https://www.gov.uk/repaying-your-
student-loan.

[14]   MoneySuperMarket, "Compare mortgagges,"
[Online]. Available:
https://www.moneysupermarket.com/mortgages/first
-time-buyers/.

[15]   Compare The Market Limited, "Mortgages," [Online].
Available:
https://www.comparethemarket.com/mortgages/.

[16]   Dot Zinc Limited, "First time buyer mortgages,"
[Online]. Available:
https://www.money.co.uk/mortgages/first-time-

buyer-mortgages.htm.

[17] Rightmove PLC, [Online]. Available:
      https://www.rightmove.co.uk/.

[18] Zoopla Limited, [Online]. Available:
      https://www.zoopla.co.uk/.

[19] OnTheMarket plc, [Online]. Available:
      https://www.onthemarket.com/.

[20] Housing & Communities, [Online]. Available:
      https://www.planningportal.co.uk/.

[21] Ofcom, "Mobile and broadband checker," [Online].
      Available: https://checker.ofcom.org.uk/en-
      gb/broadband-coverage.

[22] Uswitch Limited, "Broadband postcode checker,"
      [Online]. Available:
      https://www.uswitch.com/broadband/postcode_chec
      ker/.

[23] gov.uk, "Flood map for planning," [Online]. Available:
      https://flood-map-for-planning.service.gov.uk/.

[24] gov.uk, "Search for schools and colleges to compare,"
      [Online]. Available: https://www.compare-school-
      performance.service.gov.uk/.

[25] gov.uk EPC, "Find an energy certificate," [Online].
      Available: https://find-energy-
      certificate.digital.communities.gov.uk/.

[26] C. Jenner, Survey Your Home for Structural Building
      Defects: For Homeowners, Property Developers,

Students, Professionals and Property Purchasers, 2015.

[27] Which?, "Mortgages & property," 2021. [Online]. Available: https://www.which.co.uk/news/2021/08/cladding-crisis-new-ews1-form-advice-causing-property-market-confusion/.

[28] HM Land Registry, "HM Land Registry Open Data," [Online]. Available: https://landregistry.data.gov.uk/app/ppd.

[29] RICS, [Online]. Available: https://www.ricsfirms.com/.

[30] Law Society, "Find A Solicitor," [Online]. Available: https://solicitors.lawsociety.org.uk/.

[31] CLC, "Find a CLC Lawyer in England & Wales," [Online]. Available: https://www.clc-uk.org.uk/cms/cms.jsp?menu_id=19871.

[32] S. Vahl, "Luton man left shocked as his house is 'stolen'," 2021. [Online]. Available: https://www.bbc.co.uk/news/uk-england-essex-59069662.

[33] gov.uk SMI, "Support for Mortgage Interest (SMI)," [Online]. Available: https://www.gov.uk/support-for-mortgage-interest/what-youll-get.

[34] gov.uk, "Apply for a Council Tax discount," [Online]. Available: https://www.gov.uk/apply-for-council-tax-discount.

[35]   SpareRoom, [Online]. Available:
        https://www.spareroom.co.uk/.

[36]   Gumtree, "Property," [Online]. Available:
        https://www.gumtree.com/flats-houses.

[37]   Facebook, "Property for rent," [Online]. Available:
        https://www.facebook.com/marketplace/category/pro
        pertyrentals/.

Useful Resources

https://propertydata.co.uk/

https://www.met.police.uk/a/your-area/

https://www.crime-statistics.co.uk/

https://www.ons.gov.uk/peoplepopulationandcommunity/cr
imeandjustice/datasets/policeforceareadatatables

https://www.checkmystreet.co.uk/

propertydata.co.uk

adviceguide.org.uk

https://www.plumplot.co.uk/London-violent-crime-
statistics.html

https://www.plumplot.co.uk/London-house-prices.html

https://www.thesun.co.uk/news/14734884/crime-map-england-wales-violence-drugs-sex/

Cladding

https://www.bbc.co.uk/news/explainers-56015129

https://www.bbc.co.uk/news/business-56315729

https://www.which.co.uk/news/2021/08/cladding-crisis-new-ews1-form-advice-causing-property-market-confusion/

To avoid typing the links on your computer you can go to https://buyfirsthome.co.uk/Reference List/

Or just scan this QR code

Appendix 7: Glossary

Base Rate   The interest rate as it is set by the Bank of England, and this is the rate commercial banks are charged for loans by the central bank (Bank of England). It usually affects all other rates: mortgage, saving accounts, deposits, other loans and the rate at which penalties are calculated. When the base rate goes up, banks also increase their rates for loans, although when the interest rate goes down, they are much slower to decrease their interest rates, and they don't often drop to the same extent.

Cash buyers   Buyers who can buy without a mortgage.

CCJ   County Court Judgment for debt.

CGT   Capital Gains Tax.

Chain   The group of individuals all dependent upon on one another to sell their house so they're able to buy another one and the next person can buy theirs. If there are several sellers and buyers in the chain, it can be very difficult to manage the whole process, as all

191

purchases need to happen at the same time. If one link in the chain has a delay or a problem, the whole chain can break down. This can actually create an opportunity for the first-time buyer to get a good discount if they're ready to step in and arrange everything quickly so the other people in the chain can also buy and sell.

Completion date The date at which the purchase of the property is finalised: all money transferred, and the keys can be received. There will be some more paperwork for solicitors, but at this date the buyer can move in.

Conveyancing Transfer of a legal title of a property from one person (seller) to another (buyer).

EPC Energy Performance Certificate. It shows how efficient the property is and how much it can be improved. All properties that are sold or let are legally required to have an EPC; it's usually valid for 10 years. It's a public domain document, and when you buy a property, it's possible to download the EPC if you know the address.

Exchange contracts The point at which the buyer and the seller exchange signed contracts via solicitors. At this point, the contract to buy and sell becomes binding. Usually it's required that a 10% deposit is paid by the buyer, and this will be lost if the buyer doesn't complete the purchase.

Freehold   A type of property in the UK where the person owns the house outright together with the land on which it's built.

Freeholder   The person or legal entity who holds the legal title of the property. Freeholders are usually responsible for maintaining the building in good order.

Gazumping   When seller accepts someone's offer at a higher price for a property even though another offer has already been accepted.

Gazunder   This is when the buyer negotiates a price lower than what was previously agreed. This can happen, for example, because new information came from the survey report.

Ground rent   The payment that is required to the freeholder according to the lease. It could be a very small, fixed amount, or it could increase with time. Check it carefully; for example, some leases state that the ground rent will double every 10 years, which means that after 30-40 years the ground rent can be so huge that it will be very difficult to find a buyer and the value of the property can drop considerably.

Guarantor   This is a person—usually a family member—who agrees to pay the mortgage or other financial obligation if you can't pay yourself. With a guarantor, the bank might agree to give you a mortgage even though you don't completely meet their criteria.

Houses

Block of flats   There are wide varieties of purpose-built apartments from Victorian and Edwardian houses to modern high-rise towers. The vast majority of them are leasehold. Although some might be more affordable, some new-builds in popular areas, like central London, for example, can compete on price with more expensive houses.

Bungalow   Often detached, either single-storey or with a second storey built into a sloping roof.

Conversion flat   There are many examples where an original big house has been converted into two or more apartments. Some old conversions could be noisy because of a lack of proper insulation. More recent conversions require Building Control approval to make sure that the conversion meets certain standards.

Cottage   Small house in the country, often built with thick walls and low ceilings to preserve heat.

Detached   Stand-alone houses that are not connected to other houses. This is the most expensive type of property.

Ex-council properties   Properties that previously belonged to a local council or a housing association. Very often they provide good space and storage facilities, and if the house is situated in an up-and-coming area, this can give a good capital growth.

Link-de-tached Houses are almost detached; they don't have a common wall, but are connected via a link, often a garage.

Listed building Some buildings are recognised as being of national importance and are recorded in an official register called The List of Buildings of Special Architectural or Historic Interest. They have many more restrictions regarding what can be done with them inside and out-side.

Maisonette Apartment or flat with its own external door.

New-build property A newly-constructed property which is bought directly from the developer.

Off-plan A house that hasn't been built yet. Many developers offer good discounts so they can get the money for the construction work, but there's a big risk in case some houses are not built at all and the money is lost.

Semi-de-tached Two houses that are connected to each other with a common wall. Often the houses are similar and mirror each other.

Studio flat   An apartment with only one main room, combining a bedroom and living room. There might be a separate kitchen, or it could be an open-plan studio where the kitchen area is in the same room. Not all banks will give mortgages for studios, especially for smaller sizes. Check with your mortgage broker before going ahead, as there could be much fewer mortgage products available, and interest rates could be higher.

Terraced   Three or more houses that are connected and have common walls. There are mid-terrace and end-of-terrace houses, and they are usually cheaper than detached and semi-detached houses.

Town house   A house normally with three or more floors, with the kitchen and reception room being on different floors.

IHT   Inheritance Tax.

Lease   The contract that regulates the relationship between the freeholder and the leaseholder, states the rights and responsibilities of the parties and the payments and restrictions attached to the lease. It's a public domain document, and it can be obtained from the Land Registry if you consider buying a leasehold property.

Leasehold A type of property in the UK where the person owns the property but not the land on which it's built. The associated lease is usually set for a period of time, which can be years, and could be as long as 999 years. It's often associated with apartments, but there are also houses that are sold as a leasehold.

Leaseholder A leaseholder is a person who has signed a lease with a freeholder (landlord) to rent the land on which their house is built for a stated amount of time. People who buy apartments are often leaseholders.

Memorandum of Sale The document that is prepared by the agent after the offer is accepted. It confirms the agreed price, the address of the property and the names of the buyer and the seller, plus other relevant information.

Mortgage A loan used to buy a property and which is secured on the property. Because it's a secured loan, interest rates are much lower than for other types of loans. If you can't pay your mortgage payments, the bank can take the property from you and sell it to recover its costs. When this happens, it's often sold at a very low price so there's little or nothing left for you.

Fixed-rate mortgage A mortgage with the interest fixed for a certain period of time, typically 2-3-5 years, but there could be 10-year fixed-rate mortgages or even more. The monthly payments stay the same during this period, providing stability, but usually there is a considerable repayment charge if the borrower wants to get out of it earlier than when the fixed-rate period finishes, so it needs careful planning.

AIP Agreement in Principle is when a bank agrees to grant a borrower a mortgage, providing the property is approved.

Bridging mortgage Short-term loans that are used before the main mortgage is arranged, often to buy at property auctions. Terms could be from a couple of months to a couple of years, and they could be much more expensive.

Capital payments The proportion of the mortgage payment that decreases the amount of the loan.

Capped mortgage A variable-rate mortgage that has an interest rate that can't increase over a certain set maximum.

Discounted-rate mortgage A mortgage in which the interest is set at a discount from the SVR of the lender. It can be for a fixed period of time, like 2 or 5 years, or for the whole duration of the mortgage. The monthly mortgage payments are not fixed, and they can go up and down if the lender changes its SVR.

Equity The difference between the value of the house and the balance of the mortgage.

ERC Early Repayment Charges made by the lender when a borrower pays the mortgage in full earlier than the agreed term.

Interest-only mortgage A mortgage where only interest is paid monthly and there is no capital payment part. The mortgage amount remains the same, and you still need to repay it in full when you remortgage or sell the house. There are no longer many such products for residential houses, although the majority of BTL (Buy to Let) mortgages are interest-only.

KFI Key Facts Illustration is the document that outlines all the details of the mortgage. When a broker or lender sends it to you, check carefully if it is what you expected.

LTV A Loan-to-Value mortgage shows the maximum percentage of the value of the property that the lender is willing to lend for this mortgage product.

Mortgage term The length of time over which the mortgage is required to be paid. It used to be that most mortgages were given for 25 years, but now there are many mortgages for 30, or even 40, years. The mortgage term depends on the age of the borrower, for example, a 50-year-old person can't take a 40-year repayment mortgage.

Negative Equity
When the value of the house is less than the outstanding mortgage. It's a very dangerous situation, as the owner can be trapped with a high-interest rate and be unable to sell or remortgage without paying the difference from his own pocket.

Offset mortgage
A mortgage in which the lender opens a separate savings account for the borrower that is linked to the mortgage account. The interest of the mortgage is only calculated on the difference between the outstanding balance of the mortgage and the saving account balance, reducing the interest and cost. The advantage is that the money on this saving account is easily accessible, unlike overpayment of the mortgage for other types, and benefits are usually higher than for other instant access saving accounts.

Remortgage
Securing a new mortgage for the same property. At the end of the fixed-rate period the interest rate of the same mortgage can go up, and it makes sense to shop around for a better deal with the same bank or another. It's usually financially beneficial, even taking into account mortgage arrangement fees.

Repayment mortgage
A mortgage in which a share of borrowed capital is repaid every month together with the interest.

Reposses-sion	If the owner of the property can't pay the mortgage, the bank takes the legal owner-ship of the house and sells it to cover their costs.
SVR	Standard Variable Rate is the mortgage rate set by the lender and applied when the fixed-rate period is finished. Unfortunately, lenders can change it if the market condi-tions change, and it can be higher than it was initially planned.
Tracker mortgage	A type of variable rate mortgage which 'tracks' a base rate, often set by the Bank of England, by adding a fixed amount, for ex-ample, 0.5% or 1%. If the base rate changes, the monthly mortgage payments will change as well.
Variable-rate mortgage	A mortgage in which the interest rate can go up and down, and as a result, the monthly payments will vary. There are three types: standard variable rates (SVRs), tracker rates and discounted rates.
ONS	Office for National Statistics, the main gov-ernment source for providing statistical data in the UK.
Payday loan	Usually a relatively small amount borrowed at a very high interest rate with the agree-ment to repay it when the borrower is paid. Because of the pricey charges, it can escalate

quickly to a very high debt, which will become more and more difficult to repay. Do not take it!

Right to Buy   A government scheme by which council tenants can buy their council-owned property. Certain conditions have to be met, but it's possible to buy it at a good discount.

SDLT   Stamp Duty Land Tax, paid by buyers when they purchase houses or land in England.

Service charge   Monthly or yearly payments to the freeholder or a managing agent to maintain a building and communal areas.

Shared Ownership   "When you buy a home through a shared ownership scheme you buy a share of the property and pay rent on the rest. The share you can buy is usually between 25% and 75%. You can buy a 10% share on some homes." www.gov.uk

Subsidence   When the gradual movement of land results in structural issues with a property. If it happens, insurance for the building can go up considerably, and it might be difficult to find an insurer. It's always advisable to check in advance if the house was affected by subsidence, as this can affect the value of the property.

Index

Agreement in Principle (AIP), 84, 120, 206
auction, 100, 101
base rate, 77, 156, 199, 209
block of flats, 107, 155
Broadband, 193
Buffet, Warren, 35
Buy-To-Let (BTL), 158, 159, 160, 207
Canopy, 59
Capital Gain Tax (CGT), 160, 199
chain, 18, 45, 110, 119, 120, 122, 134, 136, 157, 200
Chaplin, Simon, 15
cladding, 99, 155, 194, 196
completion, 41, 75, 112, 117, 128, 135, 136, 138, 139, 145, 158, 175
Confucius, 125
Consumer Price Index (CPI), 68
conveyancing, 40, 129, 155
Council of Licensed Conveyancers, 128
County Court Judgement (CCJ), 54, 199

credit checks, 54, 55, 56
credit score, 36, 53, 55, 56, 57, 58, 59, 60, 61, 165
CreditLadder, 59, 192
deposit, 16, 17, 23, 24, 25, 26, 27, 28, 35, 36, 38, 39, 40, 42, 43, 49, 55, 58, 60, 65, 66, 68, 69, 70, 71, 73, 76, 80, 83, 85, 87, 91, 92, 98, 101, 122, 137, 144, 159, 169, 179, 181, 184, 185, 201
detached, 28, 202, 203, 204
Direct Debit (DD), 48, 56, 82
Early repayment Charge (ERC), 78, 207
electoral roll, 57
Energy Performance Certificate (EPC), 97, 112, 193, 200
Equifax, 53, 57, 59, 191
equity, 28, 29, 31, 68, 69, 154, 159, 180, 181, 184, 185
Experian, 53, 57, 59, 191
Facebook, 149, 195

Financial Conduct Authority (FCA), 82
fixed-term contract, 143, 144
freehold, 42
gambling sites, 83
gazumped, 133
Groom, Anne, 165
ground rent, 113, 130, 201
guarantor, 66, 202
Gumtree, 149, 194
Help to Buy, 8, 49, 67, 73
Help to Buy ISA, 49
Help-to-Buy, 8, 66
HMRC, 85, 149, 158, 175
Inheritance Tax (IHT), 161, 205
insurance, 42, 43, 58, 95, 130, 137, 138, 147, 154, 155, 156, 211
interest rate, 22, 23, 24, 25, 28, 29, 41, 47, 49, 65, 68, 76, 77, 79, 80, 81, 149, 154, 155, 156, 180, 183, 185, 199, 204, 206, 207, 208, 209, 210
Ivy Baker, 153
Japanese knotweed, 108, 109
Jenner, Chris, 99, 108
Jordan, Michael, 65
Key Facts Illustration (KFI), 207
King, Martin Luther, 22
Kiyosaki, Robert, 49
Land Registry, 114, 132, 139, 194, 205
Law Society, 128, 194
Leasehold, 205
Lifetime ISA, 49
Loan-to-Value (LTV), 23, 24, 25, 28, 65, 66, 70, 76, 80, 137, 159, 179, 180, 181, 183, 184, 185, 187, 188, 189, 190, 208
mortgage, 22, 23, 24, 25, 27, 28, 29, 30, 31, 35, 36, 38, 39, 41, 43, 46, 54, 55, 58, 60, 62, 65, 66, 68, 69, 70, 71, 72, 73, 74, 75, 76, 77, 78, 79, 80, 81, 82, 83, 84, 85, 86, 87, 91, 98, 99, 101, 109, 110, 112, 113, 117, 118, 121, 122, 126, 131, 132, 133, 134, 136, 137, 139, 145, 147, 149, 154, 156, 158, 159, 166, 169, 179, 180, 181, 183, 184, 185, 187, 188, 189, 190, 192, 194, 199, 202, 204, 206, 207, 208, 209, 210
mortgage adviser, 73, 74, 75, 78, 80, 81, 82, 84, 85, 137, 166, 169

mortgage broker, 41, 68, 75, 77, 98, 126, 169, 204

mortgage interest, 29, 62, 70, 155, 156

Mortgage Payment Protection Insurance (MPPI), 147

mould, 107, 108

negative equity, 121, 154

new-build, 25, 67, 69, 73, 97, 107, 127, 179, 202

notice period, 143

Office for National Statistics (ONS), 37, 210

overdraft, 84

Payne, Chris, 171

property ladder, 28, 35, 66, 155, 157, 158

repayment mortgage, 28, 68, 78, 180, 208

Right to buy, 67

Rightmove, 92, 93, 105, 114, 115, 159, 192

Rolih, Robert, 105

rolling periodic contract, 143

Royal Institute of Chartered Surveyors (RICS), 127, 194

secondary market, 27, 71, 73, 179

self-employed, 86, 87

semi-detached, 204

Seneca, 91

shared ownership, 71, 211

Simmons, Jennifer, 171

single-person discount, 149

snagging, 127, 166

solicitor, 40, 42, 126, 128, 129, 131, 132, 134, 135, 136, 137, 138, 139, 146, 155, 157, 166, 167, 169, 175

SpareRoom, 149, 194

Stamp Duty and Land Tax (SDLT), 9, 40, 132, 138, 158, 160, 175, 176, 210

Standard Conditions of Sale, 136

Standard Variable Rate (SVR), 207, 209

Standing Order, 47

Statista, 17, 61, 191, 192

Structural Building Defects, 99, 108, 193

student loan, 61, 62, 83, 192

studio, 16, 204

Subject to Contract (STC), 115

subsidence, 130, 211

survey, 41, 42, 100, 107, 126, 127, 128, 132, 133, 134, 156, 166, 201

TransUnion, 53, 57
valuation, 41, 80, 132, 154, 166
viewing, 97, 105, 106, 107, 108, 116, 119, 166

Which? magazine, 22, 99, 191, 193
Zoopla, 38, 92, 93, 105, 114, 115, 159, 191, 193